Women of Achievement

Abigail Adams

Women *of Achievement*

Abigail Adams

Susan B. Anthony

Tyra Banks

Clara Barton

Hillary Rodham Clinton

Marie Curie

Ellen DeGeneres

Diana, Princess of Wales

Helen Keller

Sandra Day O'Connor

Georgia O'Keeffe

Nancy Pelosi

Rachael Ray

Eleanor Roosevelt

Martha Stewart

Venus and Serena Williams

Women of ✑*Achievement*

Abigail Adams

FIRST LADY

Janet Hubbard-Brown

CHELSEA HOUSE
PUBLISHERS
An imprint of Infobase Publishing

ABIGAIL ADAMS

Copyright © 2009 by Infobase Publishing

All rights reserved. No part of this book may be reproduced or utilized in any form or by any means, electronic or mechanical, including photocopying, recording, or by any information storage or retrieval systems, without permission in writing from the publisher. For information, contact:

Chelsea House
An imprint of Infobase Publishing
132 West 31st Street
New York, NY 10001

Library of Congress Cataloging-in-Publication Data
Hubbard-Brown, Janet.
  Abigail Adams : First Lady / by Janet Hubbard-Brown.
    p. cm. — (Women of achievement)
  Includes bibliographical references and index.
  ISBN 978-1-60413-491-9 (hardcover)
  1. Adams, Abigail, 1744-1818—Juvenile literature. 2. Presidents' spouses—United States—Biography—Juvenile literature. 3. Adams, John 1735–1826—Juvenile literature. I. Title. II. Series.

  E322.1.A38H83 2009
  973.4'4092—dc22
  [B]
                                        2008055365

Chelsea House books are available at special discounts when purchased in bulk quantities for businesses, associations, institutions, or sales promotions. Please call our Special Sales Department in New York at (212) 967-8800 or (800) 322-8755.

You can find Chelsea House on the World Wide Web at http://www.chelseahouse.com

Series design by Erik Lindstrom
Cover design by Ben Peterson and Alicia Post

Printed in the United States of America

Bang EJB 10 9 8 7 6 5 4 3 2 1

This book is printed on acid-free paper.

All links and Web addresses were checked and verified to be correct at the time of publication. Because of the dynamic nature of the Web, some addresses and links may have changed since publication and may no longer be valid.

CONTENTS

One Woman's Sacrifice

On April 19, 1775, the first shots of the American Revolution were fired at Lexington and Concord. John and Abigail Adams were living in Braintree, Massachusetts. John had to return to Philadelphia and the Continental Congress. In the event of real danger, he urged his wife to "fly to the woods."[11] The woman he was issuing orders to was a little over five feet tall and had always been in frail health, although she was quick to speak her mind, even if it sometimes landed her in trouble. (The portrait artist Gilbert Stuart, who painted her when she was older, admired her dark eyes and hair and thought that in the early years of her marriage she must have been a Venus.) After John departed for Philadelphia, she, their four children, and extended family watched as American minutemen marched

A pastel portrait of Abigail Adams painted in 1766 by Benjamin Blyth. She was the wife of the second American president, John Adams, and the mother of John Quincy Adams, the sixth American president.

past their door. At the same time, refugees from Boston headed out to the village to escape the hostilities in the city. On June 17, Abigail and her mother-in-law watched the Battle of Bunker Hill from Penn's Hill near their home.

In July, the family was hit with dysentery, a potentially fatal disease. Abigail's mother arrived to help her daughter, then fell victim herself and died. The tragedy forced Abigail to call upon all her inner resources. She thought constantly about the great sacrifice her mother had made, and she felt that she was making a huge sacrifice, too, to manage so much alone. Because of the era's poor means of communications, it would be a week before John even heard the news in Philadelphia.

Abigail and John's wedding anniversary was October 25, and Abigail wrote to her friend Mercy Otis Warren, "In the 12 years we [John] and I have been married I believe we have not lived together more than six."[2] It was a hard era for raising a family. Abigail had lost a child at birth, and her daughter Susanna died at 13 months of age. Now, while John worked for American independence, she had to feed, clothe, and see to the education of their children John Quincy, Charles, Thomas, and Abigail, nicknamed Nabby. She was also responsible for the farm in Braintree and for taking care of her father and John's mother, both of whom lived close by. Meanwhile, in Philadelphia, the future of the American colonies was at stake. Abigail wrote in a letter that she could not call on John, a man "driven by profound anxiety for this future,"[3] to stay home. The truth was that both of them were committed to the work that John Adams was doing for his country and fervently believed that, without him, the new government might not fare as well.

During his absences, Abigail wrote letters to John, her "dearest friend," and the habit became a way of life for her. She wrote her husband what was in her heart, something more easily expressed in writing than in conversation. She also wrote him the latest political news from New England, information she had gleaned from legislators and friends. Though John was not able to spend much time with his children, he wrote numerous letters offering advice and instruction to Abigail, and to them.

The lengthiest separation from John came when he was appointed to France to negotiate peace with Great Britain. Abigail could not hide her dismay: "How could you contrive to rob me of all my happiness?"[4] It was difficult enough to remain in touch when they were living in the same country. Their only means of communication was letters, and it could take weeks for mail to be delivered between Braintree and Philadelphia. For her it was terrible to think of an ocean separating them. In the end, after many letters written to relatives and friends in her passionate voice, she did what she had done since they had been together—she put her country first.

John Quincy went with his father to Europe in 1778. It took two months for John's first letter to arrive in Braintree. Abigail grew discouraged. Many of the letters home never reached her, and the ones that did sometimes struck her as cold and hostile. Nabby was gone, too, living with Abigail's friend Mercy Warren as a helper; even with the two younger boys and the family servants at home, the house felt a bit empty to Abigail. Twenty-one months after leaving for Europe, John and John Quincy put into shore and walked up the hill to their home. Abigail was elated to see them. They stayed only four months, and then, on October 20, 1779, John was nominated as ambassador to Great Britain. The assignment was a great honor but also, for Abigail, a reason for dread. John decided to take both John Quincy and Charles with him this time.

They set sail on November 15, 1779. Abigail's only connection to John was their letters and the occasional news that came from men who had seen him in Europe. Abigail did not learn for some time after they arrived in Europe that 14-year-old John Quincy had been sent to Russia as secretary to the new ambassador, nor did she know that Charles, who was terribly homesick, would be returning to her. If she had known that over the next nine years she would spend only a few weeks with her husband, she might have put her foot down against his departure, the way her friend Mercy Warren had done when her husband wanted to go to Philadelphia for the Continental Congress.

The months and years of separation changed Abigail, her husband, and the lives of their children. Abigail, already quite well educated for a woman of her era, became far more independent than the average middle-class wife. She became a businesswoman and continued to run the farm successfully, even managing to buy land in Vermont. This worldy experience would help her become her husband's greatest political adviser, despite the fact that women would not even be allowed to vote until the twentieth century.

Yet she took on this role reluctantly. John pleaded with her to join him in Europe. In fact, her sister Betsy Shaw offered to take Charles and Tommy so she could make the trip. Abigail worried about what would happen to the farm and later confessed that she was terrified of the ocean. She also expressed insecurity about being presented at court. She wrote John, "A mere American as I am, unacquainted with the etiquette of courts, taught to say the thing I mean . . . I am sure I should make an awkward figure, and then it would mortify my pride if I thought I should be a disgrace

DID YOU KNOW?

Hailing from primarily English and Welsh stock, Abigail Adams could trace her ancestral roots back six centuries to royal lines in France, Germany, Belgium, Hungary, Holland, Spain, Italy, Ireland, and Switzerland. Her paternal great-grandfather, Thomas Smith, was born in 1645 in Darthmouth, England, and settled in Charleston, Massachusetts, after he arrived in America.

to you."[5] It was her daughter, Nabby, who had fallen in love with a man of questionable character, who finally prompted Abigail to set sail. She was not the first mother who tried to get her daughter away from a suitor by taking her on a trip. Nabby was 18 and had not seen her father since she was 9. Her mother was 40.

Thomas Jefferson, a dear friend and John's political ally, had hoped to escort Abigail and Nabby on their long voyage, but his offer came too late. Although she did not know it at the time, all of Abigail's patience, sacrifice, hard work, and courage would bring great rewards. In the second half of her life, she and her "dearest friend" would spend years in France and England. Little did she dream as she stood waving good-bye to the shores of America that she would one day be first lady of the land she was leaving behind.

A "Shy but Obstinate" Child

Abigail Smith Adams, born on November 22, 1744 (or November 11, according to the old-style Julian calendar), was the second of four children born to Elizabeth and the Reverend William Smith of Weymouth, Massachusetts. Her sister Mary had arrived three years earlier; her brother William, nicknamed Billy, was born two years later, followed by Elizabeth, known as Betsy, in 1750. The family lived in a comfortable, rambling house that was often overflowing with family members, servants, and friends.

Both William Smith and his wife were descended from prosperous families, though Elizabeth's family, the Quincys, was more prominent. The Quincys occupied two mansions on a hill overlooking Boston Harbor. Elizabeth's father devoted much of his life to politics and was speaker of the Massachusetts House of Representatives for many years. Though he came from a family of merchants, William went to Harvard College to become a minister. This made him part of an intellectual elite, "one of a tiny minority of men with a college degree."[1] When he felt he was financially stable, he asked for the hand of Elizabeth Quincy, who was 14 years his junior.

Abigail and her siblings had a happy upbringing in the little village of Weymouth, located 14 miles from Boston. There were complaints that their mother was sometimes too overbearing and a worrier, but their father, a good-natured man who was passionate about gardening, provided balance. Their mother, who was more formal than her husband, was considered a perfect role model as a minister's wife. She reached out to the community to help and was careful never to stir up gossip. Abigail and her sisters went with their mother on her rounds to visit the poor, where she would offer words of comfort. Elizabeth went beyond the role of a typical preacher's wife by offering spinning and weaving cloth to poor women, and even helped to market what they produced. Through her mother's example, Abigail grew up with the conviction that she had a responsibility to care for the needy.

Young Abigail tended to be sickly, but she was also feisty. Elizabeth worried about her "shy but obstinate" child,[2] who was not blessed with a gentle disposition and who was difficult to contain. Though she appeared to be reserved, her parents were aware that she often managed to get her own way. Like their peers, she and her sisters learned to sew, cook, and tend a vegetable garden, with the goal in mind that eventually they would run their own households. Two servants, Tom and Pheby, helped with domestic work, but the Smith children were still expected to help with chores.

Above, an engraved portrait of Abigail Adams, done in the late 1700s. Although considered a "shy but obstinate" little girl, she would blossom into a woman of formidable strength of character and political insight.

Everyone went to church on Sunday, which was an all-day affair. Children were expected to listen to the long sermons without fidgeting. Both of Abigail's parents were

AN UNUSUAL EDUCATION

Abigail wrote in 1778, when she was 38 years old, "Every assistance and advantage which can be procured is afforded to the Sons, whilst the daughters are wholly neglected in point of Literature."*

During her lifetime, schools were for boys. If a girl decided to go, she had to attend early in the morning and was instructed in nothing beyond basic reading and perhaps some dance and music. Working at home, Abigail was trained at an early age in reading, writing, and arithmetic. She devoured not only her father's history books and his collections of sermons, but also his complete set of *The Spectator*. The famous periodical featured essays by the brilliant author Joseph Addison; in the colonies and Addison's own Great Britain, the series was considered a model of literary style. Addison's outlook on life was enthusiastic, and he promoted moral decency and rational religion.

Still, Abigail's education happened piecemeal. She was not taught Latin or Greek, then considered the ticket to college and the professions, because the general belief was that girls had no reason to learn languages. Most girls entered their teens with the ability to write a simple letter and to read the Bible. Abigail was sensitive that her handwriting, considered the mark of an educated person, and her spelling and punctuation were not up to par.

Abigail always felt fortunate that Richard Cranch, who would marry her older sister, entered her life. Self-taught, he deeply religious and believed that God's will was the governing force in their lives. The God the Smiths worshipped, however, was not as harsh as the God of the stricter

knew the classics and classical languages, and he especially knew the Bible. He taught Abigail to love poetry. She studied William Shakespeare, John Milton, and Alexander Pope, and could quote extensively from their works. She, like many of her female acquaintances, particularly liked Pope. They were drawn to the way he gave a twist to the moral lessons that they had to learn as children. Her favorite poet was James Thomson, who "mapped the world she knew."** He taught her that "she could stand amid the opposing forces at each season of her life while still adoring the wisdom and benevolence of a perfect God fully knowable by imperfect man only in the next world."*** She was also drawn to the novels of Samuel Richardson and their themes of personal identity, duty to family and society, marriage, and the role of educated women.

Abigail believed in creating a strong intellectual foundation in youth. So firm was her belief that she was willing to send her sons abroad for long periods so they could learn about diplomacy and other cultures and languages.

---

* L.H. Butterfield, Marc Friedlaender, and Mary-Jo Kline, eds., *The Book of Abigail and John: Selected Letters of the Adams Family, 1762–1784.* Cambridge, Mass.: Harvard University Press, 1975, p. 3.
** Charles W. Akers, *Abigail Adams: A Revolutionary American Woman.* New York: Pearson Longman, 2007, p. 11.
*** Ibid.

Calvinists and revivalists. William Smith was more moderate in his views of Christianity.

Abigail spent almost as much time with her Quincy grandparents in their mansion over Boston Harbor as she did at home. This practice of sending children to live with other relations while still very young had started in the seventeenth century because people believed it would broaden a child's experience and at the same time take some of the burden off her mother. Many thought it good for the grandparents as well. Though the custom was starting to wane during Abigail's childhood, she and her siblings still managed to spend a lot of time with extended family, including her uncle and aunt, Isaac and Elizabeth Smith, in Boston. One of her favorite pastimes was to go down to the harbor to watch the boats come in. The pace at the Smiths' was faster than at the Quincys' home.

The few schools established for girls were highly inferior to those created for boys. The Smith girls were taught to read by their mother, and when they progressed to a higher stage, their father jumped in to teach them. They were introduced to their father's library at a young age and were encouraged to read whatever they wanted. Abigail often selected books that her mother felt were inappropriate for girls, but she was not prevented from reading them.

Abigail found it difficult to make friends in her hometown. She and her siblings knew almost everyone, but an unspoken social barrier separated a minister's family from his parishioners. As children, Abigail and her sisters became extremely close friends. Then, as an adolescent, Abigail spent as much time as she could in Boston, with her aunt and uncle. There she learned to make friends on her own, and on her return to Weymouth she immediately began to trade letters with them. She and Isaac, her aunt and uncle's son, tried to attain polished literary styles and improve their minds. With her girlfriends, however, Abigail could relax a bit. The girls playfully chose classical names that they used in their letters. The pen names were a way to "display one's literary attainments but also to gain—or pretend to gain—at least temporary freedom from Puritan morals and manners."[3] Abigail at first chose Diana, Roman goddess of the moon, patron of virgins and hunting, and then Portia, the "virtuous Roman matron of history and the learned woman jurist in *The Merchant of Venice*."[4] The girls, as they became women, kept using their pen names and would do so the rest of their lives. Boyfriends and husbands received names too. John Adams became Lysander, in reference to a Spartan general who died in 395 B.C., and many of his early letters address Abigail as Portia.

The young women in the Smith household, and in the community, expected to marry one day and fall into the footsteps of their mothers. There were no suitable vocations for upper-class women, and if they did not marry, they would be forced to be economically dependent on their relatives. At age 17, Abigail had her doubts about finding a husband. Though marriage to the Smith girls would bring "a good family name, a dowry of household goods, a moderate cash gift, and the distant prospect of some land,"[5] men were not lined up to court them. All three girls were educationally accomplished, and it would take men who were not insistent on traditional wives to want to marry them. Also, by the time Abigail was born, the town of Weymouth had a surplus of women.

MEETING RICHARD CRANCH AND JOHN ADAMS

Abigail's sister Mary was married at 21 to Richard Cranch, who was 36. He was a learned man, gentle, and well liked. Richard took a special interest in teaching the Smith girls, all eager to learn. Abigail, a good student, was deeply grateful to her brother-in-law. Richard's good friend John Adams had been introduced to the Smith family when Abigail was

An oil-on-canvas painting of John Adams, as he looked during the time of his presidency (1797–1801). An outspoken man with an emotional tendency, he was often seen as arrogant. Upon meeting him, Abigail thought he possessed a great intelligence and compassion.

only 15, and had not been impressed. He found the Smith girls neither "fond, nor frank, nor candid."[6] Both he and Richard had been enamored of Abigail's second cousin,

Hannah Quincy, and Adams came very close to proposing to her. After Adams began to spend more time with Cranch and the Smiths, however, he had a change of heart about the family and especially about Abigail.

Short and stout, John Adams was almost a decade Abigail's senior and had a tendency to talk too much. Some people thought him arrogant. Abigail, however, saw a man with a great heart and a strong intelligence. He, in turn, fell in love with a consistently cheerful young woman full of intelligence and wit and ready to quote the great poets. They were both deeply in love. Abigail was 20 when they were married on October 25, 1764, in the parsonage where she was born. Her father performed the ceremony.

Birthing a Nation

A month before he married Abigail, John Adams wrote to her during a troubled moment, "But you who have always softened and warmed my Heart, shall restore my Benevolence as well as my Health and Tranquility of mind."[1] His words indicate that he knew how much he would rely on her; without her he often felt unsteady. His emotions tended to get the better of him, and self-doubt often crept into his mind when life was not smooth. His mother had been unpredictable when he was a child, sometimes flying into rages, which perhaps added to his nervous disposition. To his benefit, however, his mother insisted he receive a good education, for which he was deeply grateful. He went to Harvard University, where his vast intellect and passion emerged. After commencement, he worked hard to establish his law practice, one that had begun to pay off by the time he married.

Abigail was cheerful, smart, and curious. David McCullough, in his prize-winning biography *John Adams*, notes, "She, too, loved to talk quite as much as her suitor, and as time would tell, she was no less strong-minded."[2] The newlyweds moved to Braintree (now part of Quincy), into a saltbox-style house that was only a few feet from the house where John grew up and where his mother still lived. The houses, situated on the road that ran from Plymouth to Boston, were only five miles from Abigail's childhood home and surrounded by fields. Abigail's sister Mary and her husband, Richard Cranch, lived nearby in a section of Braintree called Germantown.

John set about expanding his law practice and created an office in a corner of their house. Abigail, who rose at five every morning, went to work cooking, sewing, and gardening. Soon they had cows, sheep, chickens, and two horses. The 10-acre farm took care of most of their needs. Abigail and her mother-in-law, Susanna Adams, got along well together, much to John's relief. John and Abigail worked together on their farm, but they also spent many hours talking about Great Britain's hold on America. Both were on the road to becoming passionate patriots. A daughter they named Abigail, but nicknamed "Nabby," was born on July 14, 1765. The couple was thrilled. It was around this time that they had their portrait painted by a local artist. Bernard Bailyn, a twentieth-century historian, writes that John's face seems unimpressive in the painting but that Abigail's is "extraordinary . . . for the maturity and power of personality it expresses."[3] He concludes that it was "about as confident, controlled, and commanding a face as a woman can have and still remain feminine."[4]

RISE TO FAME

John had always been ambitious, and part of the anxiety he suffered came from that desire. He had written earlier, "I never shall shine 'til some animating occasion calls forth all my powers."[5] He wanted fame, but fame in the eighteenth century had a different meaning than it does today. Charles Akers writes in his biography of Abigail Adams that "fame denoted the qualities of greatness."[6] It included sacrifice for the common good and the ability to shape history.

The very same year Nabby was born, Great Britain began the chain of events that would bring about the moment John Adams longed for. Britain's Parliament, the body that made laws for British subjects everywhere, passed the Stamp Act. Now almost anything written or published on paper in the 13 American colonies (including all legal documents, contracts, newspapers, pamphlets, permits, playing cards, and wills) would have to carry revenue stamps purchased from the government, sometimes at steep prices. Everyone knew that the British had needed the money to pay for the cost of the French and Indian War (1754–1763), the struggle in which Great Britain had beaten France to become the top European power in North America. Even so, Americans had no representatives in Parliament, and they did not want to pay a tax that had been created without their say-so—"no taxation without representation." The Stamp Act, Britain's first attempt to tax Americans directly, triggered the colonies' first protest against taxation without representation. Eleven years later, in 1776, the issue would lead to the American Revolution.

John, who had just recently been selected as a surveyor of highways in Braintree, was angry. An essay that he wrote, *A Dissertation on the Canon and the Feudal Law*, stressed his own patriotism and what one historian called the "taproot conviction that American freedoms were not ideals still to be obtained, but rights long and firmly established by

Above, a recent photo of the Adams homestead in old Braintree, now part of Quincy, Massachusetts.

British law and by the courage and sacrifices of generations of Americans."[7] He encouraged people to think for themselves. The essay was published to much critical acclaim. The Stamp Act was repealed in 1766, a year after it had been passed, and tensions eased.

A son, John Quincy, was born on July 11, 1767, around the time John opened a Boston office for his flourishing law practice and won election as a selectman in Braintree. In April 1768, he moved his family to a rented house in Brattle Square in Boston, which then had a population of 16,000. Shortly thereafter, Abigail gave birth to another girl, named

Susanna. Although busy with domestic affairs, Abigail still found time to read four weekly newspapers on the days they were published. She also worshipped at the Brattle Street Church, attended by Boston's wealthiest families.

Baby Susanna, who had been sickly, died in 1770. John and Abigail were devastated, but their grief was eased somewhat by the birth of their son Charles, who arrived in the summer of 1770, the same year John was elected as a representative to the Massachusetts legislature. Although he would play a much more active role in politics, less money would come in. Word of his election caused Abigail to burst into a "flood of tears,"[8] but she would not hear of him refusing to serve.

It was during this period that Abigail read *Sermons to Young Women*, published by a Presbyterian minister in London named James Fordyce. The book said God created women to be helpmates to their husbands and to shoulder responsibility for the "preservation of religion and virtue."[9] The sermons encouraged women to make proper use of their intellects and recommended they read books on history, the lives of great figures, and other subjects. Fordyce's teachings affirmed the beliefs Abigail had started to form on her own.

John decided to send his family back to Braintree in 1771. After John and Abigail's son Thomas Boylston was born in September 1772, John was more focused than ever on supporting his family, and as a result he was often away, riding the legal circuit in search of cases. Abigail took over running the farm and caring for their children. Because of her often-frail health, she could not always nurse her babies for the period, approximately a year, that was expected in those days. The task that challenged her the most, though, was the need to make sure her children became "moral, God-fearing, useful adults."[10] In his book, James Fordyce instructed mothers to "rely on their own good example rather than awful admonitions."[11] Abigail worked diligently to do just that, often questioning herself.

RADICAL POLITICS

Although the Stamp Act had been defeated, Great Britain still wanted to tax the colonies. In 1767, the year after the Stamp Act was repealed, Parliament imposed taxes on a number of goods, including lead, tea, paper, and paint. Again the Americans resisted. Britain gave up all the taxes except the one on tea. In 1773, Parliament passed the Tea Act, which gave a British company the sole right to ship and sell tea to the colonies. Radical Bostonians, outraged by this taxation, took matters into their own hands and dumped British shipments of tea into the town harbor. Abigail was fully supportive, as was John, though he was miles away at the time. This action, which occurred on December 16, 1773, would come to be known as the Boston Tea Party and would prove to be a major event leading up to the American Revolution.

The British struck back and passed the Boston Port Bill, which forbade any ship to enter or leave the harbor until the town paid for the damage. To the rebels' amazement, other colonies came to the aid of Boston. The British, in retaliation, passed additional restrictive laws that created more tension.

To deal with the crisis, the colonies convened the First Continental Congress in 1774. John was chosen as a delegate by the Massachusetts General Court, and on August 10 he left for Philadelphia with his fellow delegates, Samuel Adams, Thomas Cushing, and Robert Treat Paine. Initially, John and Abigail were enthusiastic about the great honor bestowed on him. He was elated by the caliber of the colonies' other representatives, and he could not wait to tell his wife about events in the congress. Abigail began to write letters as a substitute for conversation with him. After 10 weeks, however, Abigail's letters began to express the loneliness she felt, though she made it clear that she had no doubts about the justice of their cause.

It was during this time that the Adams's servant Isaac became ill with dysentery, a dangerous disease. Next Abigail was stricken, followed by some of the children. Abigail's mother arrived to help, but became ill and died. Abigail wrote to John, "Have pitty upon me, have pitty upon me o! thou my beloved for the hand of God presseth me soar."[12] Her grief over her mother's death made her feel her husband's absence more keenly. She wrote her feelings to John, then in a later letter apologized for the distress her words might have caused him. He wrote back with great tenderness, "I tremble for you . . . If I could write as well as you, my sorrows would be as eloquent as yours, but upon my Word I cannot."[13]

REVOLUTIONARY WAR

The congress ended and John came back from Philadelphia, but the crisis with Great Britain continued. The colonies summoned a second congress, and once again John was chosen as a delegate. In March 1775, the British learned of a weapons supply depot in Concord and decided to take action. On April 18, Paul Revere rode with other men to warn of the advance of the British soldiers. The first shots of the Revolutionary War were fired the next morning at Lexington and Concord. The country people, women included, fought back; by the end of the day, the British had lost three men to every American.

Members of the Continental Congress disobeyed the king, who had outlawed public meetings, and met in May. Delegates decided to create the Continental Army, and George Washington was named as its commander. Even then, the rebels did not demand independence from British rule, just an end to oppression. The delegates sent the king an appeal, known as the Olive Branch Petition, but Britain ignored it. The mother country then sent 29,000 mercenaries to whip the colonies back into line.

Abigail and John wrote to each other as he met with Thomas Jefferson, Benjamin Franklin, Robert Livingston, and Roger Sherman to draft the Declaration of Independence, the formal statement of American independence from Great Britain. Three hundred miles away Abigail was busy with her household cares, but she tried to keep up with everything that happened politically, and she fully supported independence. After she witnessed the Battle of Bunker Hill, she learned the British had burned Charlestown, Massachusetts, occupied Boston, and imposed curfews. The city was extremely dangerous for any patriots still trapped there. Abigail prayed fervently, believing that God was on the side of the colonists, and she wrote John about her fears for the cause's future.

The women of the colonies tried to go about their daily business, which included taking on some of the responsibilities of their husbands who were busy in meetings. Many women assisted the army; Martha Washington, wife of General Washington, traveled from camp to camp with her husband. Abigail added fulltime management of the farm and household finances to the daunting job of raising the children alone.

The American army won a major victory at Fort Ticonderoga in May 1775, but failed in its invasion of Canada that December. While Washington was temporarily stationed with his troops in Cambridge, just outside of Boston, he came up with the brilliant plan of having one of his officers, Henry Knox, drag the cannons used at Fort Ticonderoga to Massachusetts, where he placed them on secretly built fortifications on Dorchester Heights. The British awoke to the sight of the cannons staring down at them, and a further glance told them that their ships could also be under fire within seconds. After a six-year occupation of Boston, the British sailed for home. Approximately a thousand loyalist families, known as Tories, returned to the British Isles with them.

DECLARATION OF INDEPENDENCE

After considerable debate, the Second Continental Congress declared independence from Britain on July 3, 1776. The following day, the Declaration of Independence, penned by Thomas Jefferson, was announced. Of the document, David McCullough writes, "It was John Adams, more than anyone, who had made it happen."[14] Abigail was elated over the news of the signing. She had reminded her husband to "remember the ladies," which became one of her most famous quotations. The underlying meaning of her request has been debated ever since. Did she want equal rights for women to be enshrined in the declaration? Or was she asking that men not have so much power over their wives? Scholars continue to debate her meaning.

Abigail was also concerned about slavery and even wondered if it had brought on the horrors of war and disease as God's punishment for America. The total population of the 13 colonies in 1776 was nearly 2,500,000, of whom 500,000 were slaves. Slavery was concentrated in the southern colonies, and Virginia had the highest number of slaves by far; George Washington and Thomas Jefferson, both Virginians, each owned approximately 200 slaves. Judge Samuel Sewall, a New Englander, had stated as early as 1700 that slavery was evil, but northerners still made great sums of money off of the ships that brought slaves from Africa to America. Even northerners who despised slavery accepted it as a political fact of life. John Adams and Dr. Benjamin Rush, a delegate from Philadelphia, both opposed slavery but went along with the Continental Congress's judgment that an attempt to end the institution would cause the southern colonies to turn against independence.

An oil-on-canvas painting of the drafting of the Declaration of Independence in 1776 by Jean Leon Jerome Ferris. Pictured from left to right are Benjamin Franklin, John Adams, and Thomas Jefferson.

The news of the signing spread quickly throughout Philadelphia. The *Pennsylvania Evening Post* printed the full text on July 5, and three days later the declaration was read aloud before an enthusiastic crowd. Bells rang throughout the day and night. People built bonfires on street corners.

The actual signing took place on August 2 in secrecy, which may be why neither Adams nor Jefferson wrote anything about it at the time. They knew they were committing treason by signing the document, and it was surely no comfort that 9,000 British troops had landed on Staten Island, New York, where they were greeted by hundreds of Tories. (In their old age, both men insisted that the date of the signing was July 4, but they were wrong.)

John Adams was appointed head of the Board of War. He wrote Abigail that he absolutely could not leave Philadelphia and was turning everything in their domestic life over to her. A week later he received her letter announcing that, because

"REMEMBER THE LADIES"

Abigail Adams wrote to John on March 31, 1776, "I long to hear that you have declared an independency—and by the way in the new Code of Laws which I suppose it will be necessary for you to make I desire that you would remember the ladies, and be more generous and favorable to them than your ancestors. Do not put such unlimited power into the hands of the husbands. Remember all men would be tyrants if they could. If particular care and attention is not paid to the ladies we are determined to foment a rebellion, and will not hold ourselves bound by any laws in which we have no voice or representation."*

It is John's playful response that has caused historians to wonder whether or not Abigail meant her words as a joke. Her husband came up with the classic put-down used by men through the centuries, namely that women already had all the power. He told Abigail that the bonds of government had been loosened everywhere with the new constitution, that blacks and Indians were now more rebellious toward their white masters and guardians, but that of an outbreak of smallpox in Boston, she had decided to put herself and the children through the smallpox inoculation. John had been through it as a younger man and knew well how uncomfortable the entire process could be. A historian describes how the doctor would make a small incision, then "with a quill scoop the pus from the ripe pustules of a patient who had the disease into the open cut. It was risky, because various purges went along with it."[15]

These were turbulent times, with war looming and the future uncertain, but Abigail Adams was secure in her belief that God was on the colonies' side in the battle for an independent nation.

"your letter was the first intimation that another tribe more numerous and powerful than all the rest were grown discontented."**

She wrote back to John, "I can not say that I think you very generous to the ladies, for whilst you are proclaiming peace and good will to men, emancipating all nations, you insist upon retaining an absolute power over wives. But you must remember that arbitrary power is like most other things which are very hard, very liable to be broken."*** Historians debate whether Abigail wanted women to be equal to men or whether she wanted men to remain as masters but with limits on their authority. Most now lean toward the second view and agree that Abigail favored male authority that did not subject women to abuse and absolute subordination, that recognized the importance of justice for all.

* Phyllis Lee Levin, *Abigail Adams: A Biography*. New York: St. Martin's Press, 2001, p. 82.
** Ibid., p.83.
*** Ibid., p. 84.

A Life in Letters

Though Abigail and John were often separated, they never grew accustomed to being apart. David McCullough writes, "It was the paradox of their lives that, as much as his public role kept them apart, he always needed to be with Abigail and she with him. She would have him no other way than he was; she believed fervently in what he was doing, encouraged him in the role, and wished no other for him; she wanted him to be where he was doing his utmost for his country. And still she desperately wanted him with her. Each worried incessantly about the other's health and well-being, at times to the point of making themselves ill."[1] As concerned as he was over state affairs, John began writing more frequently to Abigail, his letters full of his thoughts on various subjects. She had always poured out her heart to him, and his responses during this period of anxiety over the war and smallpox and domestic issues were deeply reassuring.

The couple had lived together fairly consistently during the first decade of their marriage, from 1764 to 1774, though Abigail had expressed to her friend Mercy Warren in 1776 that out of 12 years of marriage, she thought they had not lived together more than six. Abigail was by nature an optimist, but that did not mean she did not struggle with loneliness and anger. She felt at times that women were not acknowledged for their sacrifices and patriotic services. She often referred to herself as a widow or an orphan. She invariably returned to her cheerful self, however, when writing to her husband: "How often do I reflect that I hold in possession a heart equally warm with my own, and fully as susceptible of the tenderest impressions, and who even now while he is reading here, feels all I describe."[2]

AN EXTRAORDINARY CORRESPONDENT

Abigail, living in a golden age of letter writing, was gifted in her ability to convey spontaneity, intelligence, keen observation, and sincerity of expression.[3] Her voice was unique. English had undergone a change from the seventeenth century's formal style to a more naturalistic style. Letters were conversations that had all the informality of a face-to-face exchange. The approach created a bond between writer and reader and came naturally to Abigail, especially in her letters to her beloved husband, who often opened his letters to her with the salutation, "dearest Friend." Their letters, often filled with news of the day, were also love letters. Because of Abigail's acute intelligence, and her interest in her husband's activities and career, their letters are now a historian's gold mine of in-depth accounts of what happened during America's transition from colony to republic.

ABIGAIL'S FIRST FRIENDSHIP

Abigail and Mercy Otis Warren met in 1773 through their husbands. Mercy was from a powerful family in Barnstable and was married to James Warren, a farmer and politician. Both women possessed strong intellects. Mercy had shared her brothers' tutors when she was growing up, and she was pushed by her father to venture into areas that women rarely entered. Her brother James Otis was "one of the few rebels who equated American liberty with the emancipation of women."* Mercy, though she had five sons, managed to write poetry and plays and published political satire under a male pen name. Her writings were quite popular. She did not neglect her domestic duties, believing it possible to raise children and write. She was a role model for the young Abigail, who was initially a little in awe of Mercy, who was 10 years older.

Curiously, Mercy did not respond with enthusiasm to Abigail's ideas about education for women, but they shared a passion for freedom for America. The friendship between the two women cooled a little when John was due to go to France. Mercy would not allow her own husband to go as far as Philadelphia, but she wanted Abigail to put aside her fears about John's voyage to Europe. Tensions arose later when Mercy did not support the new U.S. Constitution. Later she was publicly critical of John Adams in print. He was furious and wrote letters to her that she deemed hateful. She demanded an apology, but he refused. When James Warren went to John Adams seeking a job, John was dismissive, which deepened the rift. Years later a truce was declared, and Abigail returned to writing letters to her old friend.

---

* Cokie Roberts, *Founding Mothers: The Women Who Raised Our Nation.* New York: Harper Perennial, 2005, p. 49.

Charles Akers writes, "Abigail tended to organize experience according to interesting highlights, to turn random events into a connected narrative, to judge human behavior according to some eternal truth bolstered by quotations from literary or religious figures, and to put the best possible face on her own conduct and motives."[4] It was largely through their letters that Abigail became not just her husband's wife, but his closest political ally. He trusted her judgment.

A LIFE-CHANGING DECISION

John returned to Braintree in November 1776 in desperate need of rest, as he had not been feeling well for months. By the time he left in February 1777, Abigail was pregnant. Over the next nine months, Abigail was concerned about the pregnancy. When she had a shaking fit just before giving birth, she was filled with dread. Her baby was stillborn. She was sad that Nabby would not have a sister, but she was also relieved that she survived. She wrote to John, "Join with me my dearest Friend in Gratitude to Heaven, that a life I know you value, has been spaired and carried thro Distress and danger altho the dear Infant is numbered with its ancestors."[5]

By the end of the year, John was appointed to a joint delegation in France to negotiate a treaty of alliance. It was important that America have the support of France, and it was a great honor for John to be asked. Abigail, however, was horribly upset when she opened the letter asking him to consider the position. His absences had been a challenge, but at least he was still in the country. Now he would be thousands of miles away, completely out of touch. She wrote to James Lovell, a friend who was also a Massachusetts delegate to the congress, to let him know what a hardship this would be for her family: "How could you contrive to rob me of all my happiness . . . My life will be one continued

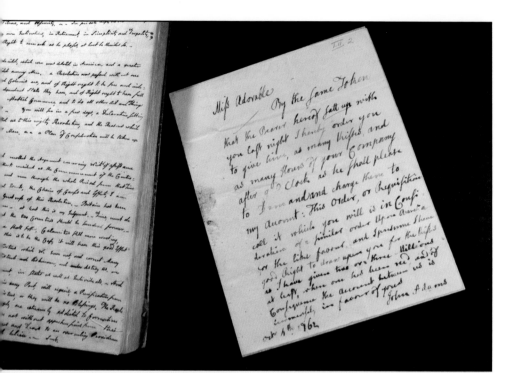

An original letter, right, from John Adams addressed to Abigail and a book of other letters written by the couple lie on a desk at the Massachusetts Historical Society in Boston, Massachusetts. The correspondence between husband and wife, which discussed many of the issues facing the young American republic, is a significant resource for historians looking at the colonial era.

scene of anxiety and apprehension, and must I cheerfully comply with the demand of my country?"[6]

America was at war. Washington had come close to suffering a terrible defeat in New York City. The British occupied Philadelphia in the fall of 1777, but soon after, General John Burgoyne surrendered to the Americans in upstate New York. Rumors flew that Boston might be invaded again. John was hopeful that France would offer military aid, but the French were wary of falling into war with Great Britain. After a flurry of letters to friends and family, Abigail concluded that her husband must take up his new post. She considered going with him and taking the family, but agreed with John that it was too dangerous to travel in wartime. John would, however, take John Quincy, then 10 years old. Abigail worried about her son being away at such an impressionable age, but she also wanted him to spend time with his father and to have a superb education.

On February 13, 1778, Abigail accompanied John to her uncle's house on Mount Wollaston in Boston, where she said good-bye. She could not bear to walk to the shoreline to wait for the small boat that would deliver father and son to the *Boston*, the ship that would take them across the Atlantic. Abigail wrote her friend Hannah Storer, "Tender as Maternal affection is, it was swallowed up in what I found a much stronger, nor had it, its full operation till after the departure of my Son when I found a larger portion of my Heart gone than I was aware of."[7]

The hours she spent writing letters became a substitute for the evenings she had enjoyed with her son and husband. It was a one-sided conversation, however, as months could pass before one of her letters reached its destination. The worry took a toll on Abigail. Rumors that the *Boston* had been captured and taken to England did not help. Abigail had almost given up when she received the news in mid-June that her husband and son were settled in France. John had not received her letters either. Abigail was so frustrated that she wrote him her anxieties, and chastised him for not corresponding more. He sent her a letter in return that expressed his upset and reminded her of the dangers that surrounded him. Abigail vowed not to write in such agitation again.

Though she hated the separation from John, Abigail had learned to cope with whatever was put before her. A new maturity had set in. She became more convinced that her husband was performing a heroic task for his country. She identified with him and his commitment, and allowed herself to feel a martyr for her great sacrifice. Akers writes, "Such self-esteem overcame any doubts concerning the value of her position in the new political order of republican America."[8]

Though she suffered from loneliness, Abigail did not lack for correspondents. A young cousin, John Thaxter Jr., was in the Continental Congress and helped to keep her informed. And another acquaintance, James Lovell, secretary of the Committee of Foreign Affairs, was happy to comply with John's request to send news to his wife. There were other correspondents, including Abigail's two sisters, and her old friend Mercy.

IN HER OWN WORDS

Some of the extraordinary letters between John and Abigail Adams were collected by editors Margaret A. Hogan and C. James Taylor in *My Dearest Friend: Letters of John and Abigail Adams*. In the following excerpt, Abigail describes to her husband the comfort letter writing brought to her during his extended absences:

> There are perticular times when I feel such an uneasiness such a restlessness, as neither company Books family Cares or any other thing will remove. My Pen is my only pleasure, and writing to you the composure of my mind.

THE CHILDREN IN 1779

Letters, however, could not replace people, especially family. Nabby was away with Abigail's friend Mercy, who was a nontraditional wife and mother. Abigail thought her spirited friend would be a good influence on her daughter, who at times seemed overly serious. Because Braintree did not have a good tutor or grammar school, Abigail had decided to send little Charles to Haverhill, where he could live with Abigail's sister Elizabeth and Elizabeth's husband. Later she would send her son Tommy to join Charles. In the meantime, Abigail took in her brother William's two-year-old daughter, Louisa. Abigail's brother had been a disappointment to the family. He had refused the opportunity to go to Harvard and now eked out his livelihood on a small farm near Abigail's. Louisa, however, was a joy to Abigail, and the hours went by more quickly as she looked after her new charge.

News from abroad remained scarce. John was impressed by Benjamin Franklin's popularity in France. He was cheered in the streets, and women copied his trademark bearskin hat. The French liked his homespun look, and he came to be seen as a typical American. Mostly, though, he was loved because he was a man of science. John respected Franklin, but not the way he chose to live. Franklin loved his pleasures and spent a great deal of money on himself. Worse, John felt caught in the middle as Franklin quarreled with Arthur Lee, their fellow envoy to France. Frustrated, Adams wrote to the Continental Congress to say that one commissioner would be enough. His letter said that commissioner was Franklin, but secretly John hoped to get the job. Instead, the congress took him at his word and John decided to go home. He had written Abigail about his concern about spies and kept many details of the negotiations from her, which caused her great frustration. Her friend

Mercy Warren, who always seemed to have knowledge of what was going on among the various statesmen, told Abigail that her husband would stay in Europe. To Abigail's amazement, on August 3, 1779, John and John Quincy showed up in a small boat that they rowed to shore. Abigail was both shocked and overjoyed to see them. Over the next few weeks, she and John took many long walks together; to her it felt like a honeymoon.

John went right to work. He represented the town of Braintree in a convention organized to frame a new state constitution for Massachusetts. The convention eventually adopted his draft of the constitution, which remains the oldest constitution continuously in use. In 1779, after he had been home just three months, the Continental Congress named John the minister plenipotentiary to Great Britain, to negotiate peace and commerce treaties. He and Abigail agreed that he had to go, but this time he took not only John Quincy but also nine-year-old Charles. It was a difficult journey. They arrived in Spain on a leaky ship named the *Sensible*, and from there they journeyed across northern Spain and over the Pyrenees to Paris.

ABIGAIL THE BUSINESSWOMAN

Abigail hated to see John and the two boys leave, but she settled down to the challenges of life without her husband. She decided to focus on finances, as the lack of money from John's political career was a constant source of annoyance to her. She made small investments, bought up land wherever she could, and found buyers for the ribbons, lace, and tea that John sent her once he was settled in Paris. At first John negotiated the prices of the European goods with merchants, but then Abigail began to write to them directly.

Mail, as always, was slow and unreliable, but Abigail did her best to keep up with developments in the Continental Congress. She, like John, was extremely protective of his reputation, and if anything came up to mar it she would be the first to jump in. As the war ground on through 1780 and well into 1781, John remained in Europe so he could negotiate the peace. Most of the fighting was now in the south, where Charleston and Savannah had fallen to the British.

John did not get along with the French foreign minister, the Comte de Vergennes, and he worried that France would have its own interests at heart when the time finally came to make peace. He decided to leave for Holland, where he could win Dutch recognition of American independence and secure loans from Amsterdam's banks. Before his trip, however, he found tutors for John Quincy and Charles because he disapproved of the harshness with which students were treated at the school where he had originally placed them.

In the meantime, Abigail stayed abreast of the news through friends in the congress and through the newspapers. The congress appointed four ministers to Europe—Benjamin Franklin, John Jay, Thomas Jefferson, and Henry Laurens. After she opened a letter that arrived at her house by mistake, Abigail learned that Benjamin Franklin had sullied John's reputation. She immediately began a campaign to support her husband.

John had little time to write to Abigail in 1781, although Abigail continued to write regularly and sent Charles and John Quincy long letters in which she urged them to excel. She did not learn for months that John had sent John Quincy to Russia as secretary to Francis Dana, who had been appointed minister to the court of Catherine the Great. Nor did she know that Charles was terribly homesick and not in good health. Concerned about his son's health, John put Charles on board the *South Carolina* with two of John's friends to look after him. The ship left in August, loaded with military supplies, but ran out of water and food and had to dock in Spain. There Charles and one of his guardians waited until they found passage on another ship, the *Cicero*, which finally brought them to Beverly, Massachusetts, in January 1782. Five months had gone by since they had left Amsterdam. Abigail had learned in September that Charles was supposed to come home, and eventually word reached her that Charles and his guardian had left Spain, but after that she knew nothing. The lack of information was a constant source of worry.

The end of the war came late in October 1781, when British forces commanded by General Lord Cornwallis surrendered at the Siege of Yorktown to American forces led by General Washington and allied French forces led by General Comte de Rochambeau. After six long years, American independence had been won. Americans were thrilled, but John and Abigail's enthusiasm was tempered by the knowledge that months lay ahead before a treaty would be signed, which meant a continued separation.

Because of the slow speed at which mail traveled, the events that Abigail wrote John about were often old news by the time her husband received her letters. She was sad to tell John of the deaths of his sister-in-law Mary and his mother's second husband, John Hall. As her children grew up, Abigail's attention returned wholeheartedly to her husband. She loved the reputation and honors he received for his role in founding the new republic, and she considered them suitable rewards for the dedication both she and John had shown.

Still, John was despondent much of the time he was in Europe. The negotiations were tedious and John worried about his reputation and what he was able to achieve. David McCullough describes how Abigail reassured her husband: "No effort was too great for peace, no cost too dear, she wrote, and he must never doubt that his own part in serving that end meant everything to her."[9] When he grew very ill and later recovered, Abigail realized that he could have died and she would not have been near him. Two years after he had been sent to Europe, Abigail wrote that she was buying land in Vermont. The news did not lift his spirits greatly, as he could not imagine ever living away from the sea, but his distance from home meant he had no choice but to put his faith in his wife's decisions.

John's spirits brightened when the Dutch recognized the United States. He went to Paris to meet his good friend John Jay. He and Jay and Benjamin Franklin now had to work together to negotiate the peace with Great Britain. After extremely difficult negotiations, the Treaty of Paris was signed on September 3, 1783. McCullough writes in his biography of John Adams, "It had been nine years since the First Continental Congress at Philadelphia, eight years since Lexington and Concord, seven since the Declaration of Independence, and more than three years since John Adams had last left home in the role of peacemaker."[10] Now Adams made it clear that he "intended never again to be separated from Abigail for any extended period for as long as he lived."[11] He wanted her to come to France.

Quest for Fame

Abigail made sacrifices that went well beyond those of many other women whose husbands were involved in colonial politics. These sacrifices were also opportunities because they allowed her, to a degree that was exceptional for the times, to demonstrate her abilities. John joked in letters about what the neighbors would say were they to become fully aware of her managerial skills.

In 1783, Abigail's father died at age 77 at the same parsonage where she was born. John pleaded with her to come to France. Abigail expressed concerns: about her health, about the danger she might face if she traveled without a protector, and about life in a new country. She had never been more than 50 miles from home, and she had a deep fear of ocean travel. On top of this, she knew that Nabby, her only daughter, had a suitor and might marry him. What she really wanted was for John to come home. She wrote at one point, "I know not whether I shall believe myself how well you Love me unless I can prevail upon you to return in the Spring."[1]

A ROMANCE IN THE FAMILY

Richard and Elizabeth ("Betsy") Cranch took in a young man named Royall Tyler. Witty, handsome, and born to a good family in Boston, Tyler had graduated from Harvard and had enough inheritance to be a possible suitor for Nabby. Although just 17, Nabby was shy, dignified, and by all standards of the day, a perfect daughter. Abigail wrote that Nabby was a "fine majestic girl who has as much dignity as a princess,"[2] but she also worried to her husband that she was perhaps too prudent and serious.

Royall Tyler reminded Abigail of John Adams when he was first starting out. She wrote to John about him and suggested that an attachment was forming between their daughter and Tyler. John was not pleased. He knew Tyler's family and was aware of the rumors that the young man had not only squandered his inheritance but fathered an illegitimate child. He complained that Tyler was known to court the mothers of young women he had his eye on. As time went by, John decided it was difficult to judge from such a distance, but he still offered his advice.

In the meantime, his letters had inspired second thoughts in Abigail. She was certain that the couple had reached a private agreement to marry, and it put her in a quandary. She overcame her fears of travel and decided that she and Nabby would go to Europe together. Tyler, who by all appearances had reformed himself, wrote to John with a formal request for Nabby's hand, but by now Abigail had made up her mind.

Charles and Tommy would stay with Abigail's sister Betsy Shaw and her husband and continue their education. Louisa, who had lived with her aunt Abigail all these years, had to return to her father's home. Abigail's uncle would be in charge of the farm and of John's mother, who lived next door. A former slave of Abigail's father's, freed at his death, would stay in the house with her husband. As the days passed, Abigail worried because she had had no further word from John. Should she go or not? After six weeks, she booked passage on the *Active;* it would sail in mid-June. John, in the meantime, sent John Quincy to London to meet them, but the boy returned to Holland after he learned that it would still be a while before they arrived.

Thomas Jefferson, now a commissioner to France, was also to sail in mid-June from New York, accompanied by his daughter Martha and a young slave. He invited Abigail and Nabby to sail with him, but Abigail had already said her farewells and did not want to change her plans. After they sailed, Tyler received a letter from John Adams giving him permission to marry Nabby.

A NEW WORLD

Abigail and Nabby boarded the ship on June 20, 1784. They had with them two servants and a cow, which was badly injured on the ship and had to be killed and tossed overboard. Abigail took it upon herself to clean the filthy ship, and in a letter to her sister Elizabeth, mentioned that she "taught the cook to dress his victuals, and have made several puddings with my own hands."[3] As the weather improved, Abigail spent hours out on the deck, watching the sea. She also spent hours with Nabby reading, writing, and playing cards.

A month later they arrived on the British coast, and from there took a post chaise, traveling 72 miles in one day. She and Nabby went to the Adelphi Hotel. Abigail was surprised to find London more pleasant than she had imagined. She dispatched a letter to John at The Hague in the Netherlands. He replied, "I am twenty years younger than I was yesterday."[4] He had some pressing business and was sending John Quincy to meet them. She went off to see a painting of John done by the famous artist John Singleton Copley and thought it "a most beautiful picture," even if she thought he had put on weight and looked a bit older. She and Nabby also went sightseeing. When John Quincy arrived, Abigail barely recognized him. He was 17 and looked older to her. Nabby was thrilled to see her father when he arrived, and for once Abigail said very little. She was too happy, and that happiness was too private to share with any of her correspondents.

OFF TO PARIS

Abigail felt she was living a page out of one of her favorite novels, *A Sentimental Journey* by Laurence Sterne, as they sped by coach-and-six across France after having sailed across the London Channel. Sterne had written, "There were all kinds of travelers . . . but the true value of travel was not in strenuous sight-seeing. It was in opening one's heart to feeling."[5]

After being ill twice, John, a great believer in fresh air and exercise, moved to a big house in the village of Auteuil, on the outskirts of Paris. The Adams family stopped in Paris first, where they met up with Thomas Jefferson and his daughter. There was talk that Jefferson would succeed Franklin as minister to France, an idea that pleased Adams. For his part, John hoped to be appointed to the British Court.

Abigail, who had lived in a cottage of seven rooms, could not believe the 50-room house John took her to. The reception room, dining room, and kitchen were on the first floor, along with the servants' quarters. The family lived upstairs, where the furnishings were sparse. Abigail thought the whole place needed a good scrub. What she fell in love with was the garden. She bought new table linens, china, and glassware and rented furniture. She hired servants, and

PARIS AND LONDON

Abigail was shocked to learn how people in Paris were judged by their display of wealth, by how many horses or servants a person possessed. The Spanish ambassador, she was told, had 75 servants. Abigail and Nabby were even expected to have their hairdresser live with them. Because their servants were ridiculed for not having their hair dressed, the Adams women felt they had to go out looking proper. Each hired person would do only what was in her job description. Abigail wrote, "To be out of fashion is more criminal than to be seen in a state of nature, to which the Parisians are not averse."*

Her first impression of the city of Paris was the filth. The buildings were black with soot and the people were the "dirtiest creatures" she had ever laid eyes on. She learned on a visit to an orphanage to which 6,000 children were delivered annually. The upper-class French seemed oblivious to such things and cared only about a good time, regularly attending the theater, concerts, and public shows of all kinds. Abigail was particularly drawn to the theater, as she had never seen a play. She could go without her husband if she wished. She grew to love the Comédie-Française and the opera.

Despite her concerns, over time she became entranced with the French lifestyle, especially with the women of fashion. She was charmed by their intelligence and the sound of their voices. The young Nabby, who kept her distance from as the warm days passed, she began to form an attachment to her new home.

Thomas Jefferson had become like family to John and Abigail and their children. The two men, Adams and

everyone, claimed that she saw her parents transformed in front of her eyes. She wrote that her mother's outlook was "more Metamorphosed" than any other aspect of the family . . . and as for her father, she "had not thought it possible, with his firmness and resolution, to be such a perfect convert to everything pertaining to dress and appearance."**

Paris had acclimated Abigail to the glamorous lifestyle of a European city, which made London easier. London was a city of extreme wealth and extravagance and extreme poverty, which was obvious everywhere they went. While there, Abigail and John went often to the theater; Abigail was thrilled to be able to see the plays of Shakespeare unfold on the stage. On the other hand, Abigail worried incessantly about finances. The cost of living was higher in London, and Abigail simply did not have the resources to provide lavish dinners. Though she thought felt more at home in London than she had in Paris, because of England's common language and more familiar customs, she grew weary of making appearances at court and longed to return to Braintree and to her other children.

* McCullough, p. 302.
** Phyllis Lee Levin, *Abigail Adams: A Biography.* New York: St. Martin's Press, 2001, p. 179.

Jefferson, could not have been more different in looks and in philosophy, but both had been vital to American independence. The bonds they formed in Paris were strong. Jefferson became like a second father to John Quincy; Nabby thought of him as an uncle.

Adams was happier than anyone had seen him in a long time. He had promised that if he could ever be with his family again he would change and not be irritable and melancholy. He was true to his word. Working with Jefferson was a joy in contrast to the struggles he had had with Benjamin Franklin. According to McCullough, Abigail confided to Jefferson that "there had seldom been anyone in her husband's life with whom he could associate with such 'perfect freedom and unreserve.'"[6] Jefferson, she wrote, was "one of the choice ones of the earth."[7] She enjoyed the attention he paid to her, and they developed their own special friendship. He had been through a series of tragedies—the loss of two children, and in 1782, the death of his 33-year-old wife, Martha, from complications following childbirth—that had devastated him. With three children left to support, he thought at the time his political career was over. Prior to his wife's death, he had achieved greatness as the author of the Declaration of Independence. As a member of the Virginia General Assembly, he wrote and revised laws that set the foundation for the former colony's new government. He had also served as governor of Virginia, a role he was glad to relinquish in 1781. When asked to go to France in May 1784, however, he accepted immediately.

Jefferson, like Franklin, spent lavishly and was constantly in debt. He thought the reason the Adams family did not sink into debt was that Adams "had the advantage of being under the direction of Mrs. Adams, one of the most estimable characters on earth, and the most attentive and honorable economists."[8] Jefferson was prone to illness and at one point told Abigail that he did not believe he would live a long life. Tragedy struck again for Jefferson when he learned that his two-year-old daughter, Patsy, had died of whooping cough. The Adams family mourned with him as Jefferson withdrew into silence.

The Adams family was living in France during the reign of Louis XVI and Queen Marie Antoinette. Along with Jefferson, who had emerged from his well of grief, Abigail and John were invited to attend one of the grandest occasions in Paris, the baptism of the king's son, the duke of Normandy. In the cathedral of Notre Dame, the Americans were given seats in a gallery overlooking the choir. The pageantry was unlike anything they had ever seen.

ENGLAND AT LAST

British-American relations were still strained after the Peace of Paris, but at last the British let it be known that they were ready to welcome an American minister. Adams desperately wanted the ambassadorship, but he did not let the congress know his desire, nor did he offer anyone else's name for consideration. Abigail was certain that he would be chosen. Although they had high hopes for John's career, Abigail and John knew the family could not stay in Europe indefinitely. They had already decided that it was time for John Quincy to return to America to complete his studies. Both he and his sister were yearning for home. Nabby had had no word from Royall Tyler, and her future was up in the air. Abigail also experienced waves of homesickness. "What a sad misfortune it is to have the body in one place and the soul in another," she wrote her sister Mary.[9] After living in a foreign country, she respected her husband all the more for living alone for so long among people he did not know.

On April 26, Jefferson rode out to their home to deliver a letter announcing that John had been appointed minister to the Court of St. James, as the ambassadorship to Great Britain was called. He had to be there by June 4. Jefferson was to replace Franklin in France. The thought of leaving France, and Jefferson, made the family sad. Each of them had developed a special friendship with Jefferson, including Abigail. Charles Akers, in his biography of Abigail, notes: "The Virginian had probably never before known a woman so nearly his intellectual equal with whom he could discuss such topics as literature and foreign policy, as well as the proper management of a household."[10]

The nine-month stay in Paris had bolstered Abigail's confidence. On a more superficial level, she had come to dress in a more sophisticated style and had developed new manners that would remain with her the rest of her life. The journey to London was uneventful. Abigail and John were entering the city with some anxiety over how they would be accepted; as the American minister, John would be testing the post-revolutionary strength of the new country, and there was bound to be some resistance from British Tories and exiled American loyalists.

The population of London was then approximately one million. The great dome of St. Paul's Cathedral loomed over the city. London was both the British Empire's political capital and its center of finance, manufacturing, and trade. The Thames carried more traffic than any other river in Europe. The metropolis was fast paced, a huge magnet for the young. What Abigail loved most about the city was the entertainments, with theater being her favorite. She and John and Nabby also attended church regularly. As former colonists of the British Empire, the Adams family did not feel welcomed in England; in fact, they were often ignored. Very few British women called on Abigail, and the one who did, the wife of a member of Parliament, asked, "But surely you prefer this country to America?"[11] They enjoyed the company of the American painters Benjamin West and John Singleton Copley and of the artists' protégés, Mather Brown of Massachusetts and John Trumbull of Connecticut. Both

John and Abigail had their portraits painted. The painters, it turned out, had an influence at court that turned out to be a great help to John.

Since John was now a major public figure, Abigail felt the demands of his assignment more than she ever had in the past. She helped him emotionally when things went badly, and she became a keen observer of his associates. As always, she was the defender of his reputation. He needed her support tremendously, for he was often attacked in the press, called an imposter and a nobody. David McCullough writes, "The *Public Advertiser* reminded its readers that all so-called American patriots were cowards, murderers, and traitors." According to McCullough, Jefferson was stunned by the slander and wrote Abigail, "Indeed a man must be of rock who can stand all this."[12]

John was officially presented to King George III in late June. He was surprised at how cordial their first meeting was. All three members of the family were invited to the queen's circle, along with Colonel William Stephens Smith, who had been appointed by the Continental Congress as secretary of the American delegation. Abigail and Nabby spent days preparing; when it was all over, Abigail delivered a humorous account of the event to her sister. She did not find Queen Charlotte pretty in the least, and wrote Mary that the ladies of the court were "very plain, ill-shaped, and ugly, but don't tell anybody that I say so."[13] Abigail learned later that she was expected to appear at the queen's weekly receptions, which meant buying new dresses.

Abigail went house hunting, and finally found one on Grosvenor Square that the family could afford. John ordered his furniture to be moved from the Netherlands. Abigail found prices in London to be very high. When told that she would need 11 servants, she settled for 8, yet discovered, just as in France, that no servant would take on the work of another. She and John put on weight when

A full-length portrait of King George III (1738–1820) in his military uniform, done by William Beechey circa 1800. During John Adams's time as ambassador to Great Britain, both he and Abigail did not feel welcome in London, since they were both former colonists of the British Empire.

they started following the local custom of eating twice a day, a late breakfast and then dinner between four and six. Abigail's social isolation had lessened, but she found paying and receiving calls dull and felt alone in gatherings of women. Most of her friends were fellow Americans.

John and Abigail were thrilled when Jefferson arrived in March 1786. Elegant in attire and manner, he drew attention everywhere they went, though he had little patience for the rudeness of the British. Abigail hosted several dinners in his honor, and the old friends went to the theater often. On a trip to visit various towns in England, Jefferson and John cemented their friendship and were reminded of their many common interests. Jefferson later wrote to his friend James Madison about John, "He is vain, irritable and a bad calculator of the force and probable effect of the motives which govern men. This is all the ill which can be said of him . . . he is so amiable that I pronounce you will love him if ever you become acquainted with him."[14]

NABBY MEETS HER HUSBAND

After Nabby officially broke off her engagement with Royall Tyler, who had been negligent in his business dealings, she began seeing Colonel William Smith. Their interest in each other had been apparent for months. Abigail wanted her daughter to be sure of her desire to marry, and Nabby declared that she was. On June 12, 1786, she and Smith were married in a small ceremony at the Adams home. At first they stayed with Abigail and John, but eventually the young couple moved into a house on Wimpole Street. The separation from her daughter was hard on Abigail. She wanted Nabby and Smith to come to dinner every day.

John was working harder than ever and spent increasing amounts of time alone. Abigail felt lonesome, she confessed to her sister. She and John went on a vacation to The Hague in the Netherlands and took Nabby and her husband with them. It was refreshing to be in a clean and orderly country where they felt appreciated. Upon their return, they learned that Nabby was pregnant.

A baby boy was born to Nabby and William on April 2, 1787. Abigail was elated. This was followed by a visit from Jefferson's daughter Polly, who was accompanied by a slave named Sally Hemings, who was only 14. (Rumors would later abound that Jefferson had children by the young Hemings, but John and Abigail chose to ignore them.) Both John and Abigail were won over by little Polly, who had lived with her aunt since her mother died. In fact, Polly and Abigail formed such an attachment that both cried when Jefferson's valet came to take Polly home.

Jefferson later wrote to Abigail, "I have considered you while in London as my neighbor, and look forward to the moment of your departure from thence as to an epoch of much regret and concern to me . . . My daughters join me in affectionate adieus."[15] Abigail wrote back thanking him for his kindness and friendship toward her and her family.

After three years in England, it was time for John and Abigail to return to America and to a much grander house than they had lived in before. John had heard that the "Vassall-Borland place" in Braintree was for sale and arranged for Abigail's uncle, Cotton Tufts, to purchase it. It included 80 acres and various farm buildings. In the midst of all her packing, Abigail received a letter that her brother, William, had died. She was deeply sad but could not stop to grieve.

John was anxious for the day when they would arrive in Braintree and begin a quieter life. Nabby, writing to her brother John Quincy, claimed that a rumor was spreading across Europe that their father would be elected vice president. Abigail, weary of the duties they had been performing, wrote

An oil portrait of Abigail Adams, done by Mather Brown in 1785, which shows how she looked during her time in England.

that any further role in politics might be "a little like getting out of the frying pan and into the fire."[16]

John had not been home in a decade, except for the few months he had with his family in 1779. He knew that his years as a diplomat were over, and Abigail could not wait to return home and see her sisters and her younger boys once again. Underneath, however, both likely knew that their work for their country would continue. Their commitment to America had been reinforced by the years abroad. Abigail considered their country a "near paradise" compared to England, where "freedom meant only the liberty of the upper classes to oppress the poor."[17]

The Vice Presidency

John and Abigail could not believe their eyes as their ship, the *Lucretia*, sailed past the lighthouse that stood about 10 miles north of Boston. The lighthouse had particular significance because it had been rebuilt after being destroyed by the British in 1776. The keeper of the lighthouse, John Knox, signaled others who were waiting on Castle Island, and a cannon boomed to alert the townspeople. Knox then rushed to Boston's port to give John and Abigail Adams an official welcome from Governor John Hancock. Several thousand people had gathered to welcome the ambassador. Church bells rang out. More cannons sounded.

Although John and Abigail were overjoyed to see their sons, Charles and Thomas, who were now 18 and 15, and John Quincy, who had turned 21, their new house needed repair. Abigail set right to work. John, however, did not jump back into his own work, politics. It was 1789 and the nation had a new constitution, the same one that has guided the United States ever since. Now the new government had to be filled. John abided by the unstated rule that one did not show ambition or chase after positions of authority. While talk swirled around New England political circles about what his future role might be, he immersed himself in farming. He was hopeful, however, and had decided that vice president was the only position he would accept. The highest post of all, president, was bound to go to George Washington, the general who had led the Continental Army to victory in the revolution.

America had changed in the years John and Abigail had lived abroad. Young men had replaced many of the older politicians. The Treaty of Paris had doubled the size of the nation, whose western border now extended to the Mississippi River, and the population was expanding rapidly. People were moving west, to territories like Ohio, Kentucky, and Tennessee. Still, Philadelphia remained the largest city, with a population of 40,000, and Virginia remained the richest, most populous, and most politically powerful of the 13 former colonies. Washington was from Virginia, so it made sense to have a northerner as vice president, for balance. Whether Adams should be that northerner was another question. He was known for being "blunt, stubborn, opinionated, vain, and given to jealousy."[1] On the other hand, he was brilliant and had proven himself to be an outstanding negotiator.

Under the new constitution, the different states' legislatures chose 69 men who would vote for president. Each of these men, called electors, named two choices for the office. Whoever received the most votes became president, and whoever came in second became vice president. Washington received 69 votes and was unanimously elected.

John came in second, but a much more distant second than he had expected. Washington's clever young ally, Alexander Hamilton wanted to avoid even the remotest chance of a tie with Washington, so he persuaded political leaders not to bunch their support behind John. Instead, they scattered their second-choice votes between John and nine other candidates. Of these votes, John received fewer than half.

Jefferson wrote Adams a note of consolation: "No man on earth pays more cordial homage to your worth or wishes more fervently your happiness."[2] John, now 53, was given a hero's farewell when he left Quincy to travel to New York, where the seat of the new national government was located. The weather was ideal for his weeklong journey, and people lined the sides of the road to see the new vice president. Abigail had decided to remain at home until he found a house for them in New York. She was happy to be with family and friends.

LIFE IN NEW YORK

The office of the vice president, however, did not suit John Adams. Adams carried out the few official duties of his office with his usual commitment, but Washington rarely consulted him. Part of the problem was that Adams had been accused of being a monarchist after the publication of his work *A Defence of the Constitutions of Government of the United States of America*. He vehemently denied being a monarchist, but he had already convinced many people that he was one by insisting that the president of the United States and those serving with him be given lofty titles. Jefferson was among the first to scoff at such nonsense.

John and Abigail believed in a strong national government. They felt it important that high titles be bestowed on officials and that the officials should live in exalted fashion, to match their importance to the country. They believed these things created respect for leaders among citizens. It is likely that some of this belief was based on their personal experience. Why would anyone want to run for office if they had to sacrifice the way Abigail and John had? Other Americans disagreed. They believed that central government must not be placed at a great height above the people. After all, they said, America had fought a war to get away from monarchy and did not want an imitation of it.

Despite the difficulties of the vice presidency, Abigail and John were happy in their domestic life. John rented a house in Richmond Hill that overlooked the Hudson River. After the years in Europe, Abigail found that running a household of 18 and attending to social obligations came easily to her. New York seemed dull after Paris and London, but she liked being in the middle of the political arena. "I am fearful of touching upon political subjects," she wrote. "Yet perhaps there is no person who feels more interested in them."[3] It was upsetting to her to learn that Congress had voted the president a salary of $25,000 and just $5,000 for the vice president. The good news for the new government was that Jefferson had accepted the appointment to be Washington's secretary of state, and that John Jay had been appointed chief justice of the Supreme Court.

Washington had created a government of revolutionaries, the men who had defeated the British Empire. Now these illustrious gentlemen struggled to make common cause as they faced life after victory. Over the next few years they would divide into two groups. The Federalists, who included John and Abigail Adams, believed in a strong central government that could protect property and order. The Republicans, led by Thomas Jefferson, believed that ordinary citizens had to be protected against domination by the wealthy and powerful. The Federalists wanted to build up the central government's authority; the Republicans wanted a government that would never be more powerful than the people it governed, one that would be dominated by the states instead of being able to dominate them. (Jefferson's party, eventually called the Democratic Republicans, is the ancestor of today's Democratic Party. The present-day Republican Party actually began in the 1850s.)

Even before the Federalist and Republican factions emerged, the argument about strong government versus weak government had caused tension for some time. The former colonies had been reluctant to submit to a central authority, so their first try at a national government let the individual states keep most of the power. That arrangement, known as the Articles of Confederation, proved fragile, and in 1787 representatives from the states began work on revising it. The result was a new document, the Constitution of the United States of America, which created a stronger federal government; more than 200 years later, it is still the country's fundamental law, the blueprint that sets out what the national government can do and the rules it has to follow. Supporters of the Constitution, like John and Abigail, believed it would allow the country to be governed effectively without the creation of a tyranny. Opponents, including Abigail's old friend Mercy Warren and Mercy's husband, were not convinced. The relationship between the two women became difficult when John, as vice president, refused to secure a position in the government for James Warren.

Too often, the fundamental questions that faced the young country would place John and Abigail at odds with old friends. Three issues soon pushed to the fore.

THE FRENCH REVOLUTION

In 1789, the same year that America's new constitution took effect, the French people began to shake the foundations of their country's monarchy. It was the start of the French Revolution. Within four years, the French would overthrow their monarchy, establish a republic, execute

A full-length portrait of Louis XVI, King of France, by Antoine-Francois Callet. The king is shown here in his coronation robes; he died under the guillotine in 1793, during the French Revolution.

their king, and go to war against some of Europe's greatest monarchies. In 1793, Great Britain joined the war against France—which presented the United States with a problem. The treaty America had signed with France in 1778 required the two countries to help each other if either had to fight Britain. President Washington, repulsed by the excess of the French Revolution, declared a policy of American neutrality in the war.

The American people, however, were divided. On the one hand, many believed the American Revolution had not gone far enough and that now France showed the way toward true equality for all. Others, like Abigail, worried that revolutions could go too far, that a chase after absolute liberty and equality would produce tyranny. They noted how the French revolutionaries executed anyone even suspected of being an enemy of the new order. Abigail had grown to believe that ordinary men and women were not able to think rationally about important issues. She thought that the violence overwhelming France showed that men of education and understanding had to hold the emotions of the people in check.

On the other hand, Thomas Jefferson was a firm supporter of the French Revolution and had many supporters within the government. Abigail considered Jefferson's views dangerous. Misunderstandings occurred between Jefferson and Adams after their opinions were published, even when their names were disguised in print. Their politics made them grow apart. Jefferson had less and less to do with Adams, but both men remained cordial in social situations. Neither wanted to end their friendship.

ESTABLISHING THE CAPITAL AND ASSUMING DEBT

A major issue facing the Washington administration was where to locate the new government. New York politicians were lobbying to keep it in New York, but others wanted Philadelphia. (Ultimately, the capital would be established in a federal district on the Potomac River, today known as Washington, D.C.) In his capacity as vice president, Adams cast the tiebreaking vote in the Senate that made Philadelphia the new temporary capital until the permanent capital could be built. (According to the Constitution, the vice president presides over the Senate but votes only in the event of a tie.) Abigail was unhappy about leaving Richmond Hill for Philadelphia since her third grandson had just been born. After she and John moved into a brick house two miles out of Philadelphia, her social life intensified. As the wife of the vice president, she had to pay calls and accept visitors on a continual basis, even though she suffered from rheumatism and her general constitution was weak. John, on the other hand, had remained in robust health throughout their travels and transitions.

Another crisis facing the new government occurred when Secretary of the Treasury Alexander Hamilton, a man admired by Adams and despised by Jefferson, wanted the federal government to pay off state debts, which would give the federal government considerably more power since it would be in charge of the entire nation's financial obligations. Such a move was violently opposed by people who wanted to keep power with the states, especially southerners. Then in 1791, debates erupted over the establishment of a monetary system. Hamilton supported strengthening the federal government by levying import duties, which made him even more unpopular with supporters of states' rights. Ultimately, however, Hamilton got his wish.

Despite the problems facing the country, Abigail was optimistic about the new government. Every state had ratified the new constitution by the winter of 1791. Things were also looking up on the home front: Nabby's husband, Colonel William Smith, was appointed supervisor of the federal excise for the state of New York, which was a big relief to Abigail and John, as they never ceased to worry about Nabby's status as wife to a man who seemingly could not hold a job.

At 48, Abigail found herself taking stock of her life; in addition to looking back at her family's role in the formation of America, she looked ahead to further developments in her husband's political career, despite her health issues. Because she continued to suffer from intermittent fevers and a general malaise each time they were due to return to Philadelphia, she stayed in Massachusetts throughout John's second term as vice president, but she kept up with everything that was happening politically.

The country's second presidential election took place in November 1792. Around that time, John began to ruminate on their life together and apart. He wrote Abigail, "Our attachment to Character, Reputation and Fame increase I believe with our years."[4]

THE ADAMS CHILDREN

The children were a concern for Abigail. Nabby's husband had not gone into law as her John had advised him to do.

IN HER OWN WORDS

In addition to supporting his political career, Abigail Adams had come to share in her husband's quest for fame. According to Phyllis Lee Levin's biography, Abigail once wrote to John:

> I know the voice of Fame to be mere weathercock, unstable as Water and fleeting as Shadow. Yet I have pride, I know I have a large portion of it.

He was constantly changing jobs, and money was tight. John Quincy had finished at Harvard and, following in his father's footsteps, had established a law office in Newburyport. There he met a young woman named Mary Frazier whom he wanted to marry, but he was still financially dependent on his parents. Abigail advised him against marrying until he was able to support his wife. John Quincy dutifully obeyed, but he was unhappy about his decision.

Tommy caused his parents few headaches. Charles, on the other hand, made Abigail fret. The most outgoing and charming of the Adams boys, he had kept bad company at Harvard. When he was out drinking with a group of friends, some of them stripped down and ran naked through Harvard Yard. One student was expelled, others reprimanded. After graduation Charles moved with his parents to New York, where they could keep an eye on him, but he refused to go along when they moved to Philadelphia. Instead he lived with his sister and her family.

REELECTION

By the time of the 1792 election, the battle lines between Federalist and Republican had grown clear. Thomas Jefferson led the Republicans with James Madison, his close friend from Virginia who had penned most of the Constitution. Washington and Hamilton led the Federalists. Even though John and Abigail sided with the Federalists, the two of them hated to see Americans divided into political parties.

With Abigail in Quincy most of the time and John in Philadelphia, they began writing each other regularly again. Abigail wrote to him in January 1793: "My days of anxiety have indeed been many and painful in years past, when I had many terrors that encompassed me around. I have happily surmounted them, but I do not find that I am less solicitous to hear constantly from you than in times of more danger."[5]

The demolition of the Bastille in July 1789, as portrayed by Jean-Pierre Houel. The French Revolution would have a profound impact, not only in Europe, but also in the United States.

Although Washington was very popular and assured of reelection, John had to fight to keep his office. Despite their best efforts, the Republicans failed to unseat him as vice president. On March 4, 1793, Washington and Adams again took the oath of office. John's excitement about the new term in office was tempered by the news that the French had beheaded Louis XVI on January 21. Not long after, Great Britain and Spain declared war on France in early 1793.

The bad news seemed relentless. The Reign of Terror had started in France, the goal of which was to purge France of the enemies of the revolution and protect the country from

foreign invaders. Estimates vary of the number of French citizens put to their death, with the high being around 40,000.
Near the end of 1793, the French executed their former
queen, Marie Antoinette. Abigail was horrified to learn soon
after that the grandmother, mother, and sister of her friend
Madame Adrienne Lafayette had also been killed. Things
were not much better at home. In Philadelphia, an outbreak
of yellow fever had killed 5,000 people.

Around this time, Adams sent Jefferson the gift of a book.
It was the first time he had written his old friend in more
than two years. Jefferson replied, enthusiastically writing
about his love of farming. They sent notes back and forth
over the next two years. In part because of this correspondence, Abigail thought she sensed more general acceptance
in her husband.

Both she and John were elated when John Quincy was
nominated by President Washington to be the minister to
the Netherlands, but this professional success was tinged
by personal disappointment. They were not happy to learn
that Charles had fallen in love with Sally Smith, the sister of Nabby's husband, Colonel Smith. Abigail and John
objected, but later learned that the couple had been married
in New York.

PRESIDENT OF THE UNITED STATES

Abigail and John had often speculated about John becoming
president. Washington had mentioned to John several times
that he wanted to retire and refused to serve a third term.
In September 1796, the president's Farewell Address was
published in many American newspapers. Abigail wrote that
were it for her alone to decide, she would advise John not
to follow Washington into the presidency. "I can say only
that circumstances must govern you," she wrote, "[and]
pray that you have superior direction."[6] If there were a new
president, she certainly did not want John to continue as

vice president. She advised him to be "second under no man but Washington."[7]

John told Abigail he did not know how he could live without politics, but he also confessed to being tired of the political game. She wrote back, "You know what is before you—the whips, the scorpions, the thorns without roses, the dangers, anxieties, the weight of empire."[8] Along with all those hazards, she believed, there waited the presidency, a "glorious reward" for all his service to his country.

Around this time, the Jay Treaty, negotiated by John Jay to resolve the issues remaining with Great Britain left over from the American Revolution, divided political leaders in the United States. Although the agreement increased trade and averted war with Great Britain and was approved by President Washington, Jefferson, Madison, and their supporters, who feared it would strengthen the Federalists, opposed it. After the Senate approved the treaty, a new optimism set in.

John requested a leave of absence and went home, his term as vice president virtually over. Abigail's health was better, and they settled in together on the farm once again. Politics seemed in the far-distant past, yet the future loomed large as the days went by. In 1796, it would be time to elect a new president.

Second First Lady

In the run-up to the election of 1796, Adams and Jefferson were considered the leading candidates for president. While they remained at their respective farms, Jefferson at Monticello and Adams at Peacefield, an all-out political battle was occurring, much of it waged through the extremely partisan newspapers. The accusations bordered on slander. For example, Adams was presented as a "gross and shameless" monarchist and unfit to lead the country.[1] Alexander Hamilton was also exerting his influence behind the scenes, urging support for Thomas Pinckney for president, a man he thought he could control. When Abigail and John learned of what he was up to, Abigail privately compared him to Cassius, the man who had betrayed Julius Caesar. Both labeled him a hypocrite.

On November 23, 1796, when the votes had been cast but not yet counted, John said good-bye to Abigail; with his servant John Briesler as his only companion, he arrived in Philadelphia 11 days later. He was under a great deal of stress waiting for the election to be over. The final count would not be known until February, but he wrote Abigail to tell her that it was being said openly that he would win. Jefferson, when told by his friend James Madison that he must accept the vice presidency if matters came to that, replied, "He [Adams] has always been my senior, from the commencement of my public life."[2]

Adams won. Jefferson wrote to his old friend, "No one will congratulate you with purer disinterestedness than myself." He added that he hoped "that your administration may be filled with glory and happiness to yourself and advantage to us is the sincere wish of one who though, in the course of our voyage through life, various little incidents have happened or been contrived to separate us, retains still for you the solid esteem of the moments when we were working for our independence, and sentiments of respect and affectionate attachment."[3]

David McCullough writes of the letter, "It was . . . one of the warmest expressions of friendship Jefferson ever wrote or that anyone had ever addressed to Adams."[4] Interestingly, Jefferson decided to have his friend Madison read it first, who insisted that it not be sent. Madison felt that if Adams failed as president, it could be politically embarrassing for the public to see such confidence in him from Jefferson.

Abigail had her own friendship with her husband's rival and could not erase him from their lives. Admitting that Jefferson had made mistakes, she wrote, "I do not think him an insincere or corruptible man. My friendship for him has ever been unshaken."[5]

TORN BETWEEN TWO WORLDS

The inauguration of John Adams took place on March 4, 1797. By the time he became the second president of the United States, the nation had grown from the original 13 to 16 states; the new additions were Vermont, Kentucky, and Tennessee. Unfortunately, not one of his family members was there to witness it. Though he felt alone, the entire day was a tremendous success, and Adams, for once, was praised by one and all for his speech and the way he conducted himself. John wrote to Abigail later to say that his inaugural was "the most affecting and overpowering scene I ever acted in."[6]

John implored Abigail to come as soon as she could. He stated that he could not manage the presidency without her advice. His letters were cajoling, complaining; he was adamant that he could not be president without her. When she had still not committed, he wrote, "I can do nothing without you. We must resign everything but our public duties."[7] He even told her to forget about the farm.

The woman he could not manage without was then nursing his mother, who was ill, as well as a niece who was unwell. Abigail had worked hard for many years to maintain the farm, and was not about to give it up, even with his permission. She was torn. Another letter came from John, telling her that "It seems to me that the Mother and Daughter ought to think a little of the President as well as the Husband."[8]

As president, Adams was deeply concerned about how to handle France. The United States had been having increasing troubles with the French republic since Britain and America had signed the Jay Treaty in 1794. Adams did not want to go to war, but France was seizing U.S. ships because the French believed that the United States was behaving favorably toward the British, with whom the French were warring. Despite its declaration of neutrality in the war between France and Britain, the United States continued to have its trade with Britain disrupted by France.

Abigail was with John's mother when she died on April 1797 at the age of 89. She wrote to her husband and made arrangements for the funeral. She departed Quincy for Philadelphia in late April with servants and relatives in tow. On her way, she stopped to visit Nabby in New Jersey and was greeted by a tearful daughter who did not know where her husband was.

ROLE OF FIRST LADY

As first lady, Abigail became the number one hostess in the country. She followed in the footsteps of Martha Washington, holding receptions and gatherings where politicians and local people could meet. Despite her best efforts, she was soon criticized for her formality and starchy personality. Martha Washington had set a tone that was elegant enough to impress foreign dignitaries and yet open enough to satisfy the people of the new republic. The personalities of the two first ladies could not have been more different. while Martha was a charming southern woman, adored by the masses, Abigail was often blunt-spoken and a no-nonsense type.

She loved politics, and she was soon consumed by affairs of government. A thorn in her side was Benjamin Franklin's grandson, Benjamin Franklin Bache, publisher of a radical printing press that had been left to him by his grandfather. Bache heaped abuse on John, which infuriated Abigail. She grew to hate the popular press, but in a free society was powerless about what was written. She relieved her tension by writing to her sister Mary of all the goings-on. Her letters to Mary covered a wide range of subjects, switching from the possibility of war with France to fashion and the lives of her children. Abigail's biggest personal news of the moment was that John Quincy, at age 30, married Louisa Catherine

Johnson, the daughter of the U.S. consul in London, on July 26, 1797, with his brother Thomas at his side.

Cokie Roberts, author of *Ladies of Liberty*, writes that Abigail "had always been ambitious for John, had been eager for him to hold the highest office, but this was a tougher job than Abigail had any reason to expect."[9] The day before the inauguration, John had consulted with Jefferson about forming a bipartisan trio to send to Europe to help stave off war. Adams said he wanted to send James Madison. Jefferson thought his friend would not accept but agreed to ask him. When John consulted his political allies about sending Madison to Europe, he was met with strong resistance. Jefferson and Adams met after a dinner following the inauguration, and Jefferson said that Madison had

IN HER OWN WORDS

Although Abigail Adams was always her husband's greatest supporter, she did not relish the idea of becoming first lady or enjoy the types of criticisms her husband had to endure from the press or his political enemies. Following his election to the presidency in 1796, she wrote shortly before joining her husband in the capital, as quoted by Charles W. Akers in *Abigail Adams: A Revolutionary American Woman*:

> At my age, and with my bodily infirmities, I shall be happier at Quincy. Neither my habits, nor my education or inclinations, have led me to an expensive style of living, so that on that score I have little to mourn over. If I did not rise with dignity, I can at least fall with ease, which is the more difficult task.

no interest in going. Adams offered that it was not possible anyhow. It was clear to both men that cooperation did not exist on either side. Jefferson always maintained that it was at that moment that they reached a breaking point.

WAR WITHIN AND WITHOUT

Europe was in turmoil. French generals, Napoleon Bonaparte foremost among them, had spread revolution to France's neighbors and even threatened Great Britain. When John's team of envoys—John Marshall, Elbridge Gerry, and Charles Pinckney—arrived in France, the government there refused to accept them unless the United States paid a hefty amount of money. Through three agents, the foreign minister, Charles-Maurice de Talleyrand, escalated his demands until the price of recognition was a multimillion dollar loan to France and a quarter-of-a-million dollars in Talleyrand's pocket. After Pinckney refused, both he and Marshall asked for passports home. At the same time, Gerry had been secretly negotiating with Talleyrand, who knew he was pro-French and thought he could be influential back in the United States. When Adams eventually made this incident public in his report to Congress, it became known as the XYZ Affair, because the president substituted the letters X, Y, and Z for the names of the three French agents—Conrad Hottinguer (X), Pierre Bellamy (Y), and Lucien Hauteval (Z)—who had approached the American delegation with the bribe offer from Talleyrand.

Abigail was shocked to hear what was going on. Cokie Roberts writes, "Abigail was in a state of constant fury. She was mad at the voters for sending Republicans to Congress, mad at Congress for its pro-French sympathies, mad at Jefferson for undermining the president, mad at the press for its attacks on her husband, and mad at the people of Philadelphia for throwing a party for George Washington's birthday."[10] In fact, the first lady was hopeful that Congress would declare war against the French. Abigail wrote in a letter, "France can pour in her armies upon us, and spread her depravity of manners, her Atheism in every part of the United States."[11] Her views became well known. One Republican politician referred to her as "Mrs. President, not of the United States but of a faction."[12]

Just as today, partisan politics were strong in 1798. The Federalists continued to put their faith in a strong central government. The Republicans remained pro-French and supportive of states' rights. The Republicans, suspicious that the Federalists were exaggerating what was happening in France, insisted that the reports from the envoys in Paris be made public. President Adams had initially held back information because he wanted to first make sure that his envoys were safe. The House of Representatives stepped in and passed a resolution that the president had to release the reports. He did. Abigail had a moment to gloat, for the pro-French Republicans were shocked to discover that the French demands for briberies from American representatives were true. After that, the American public switched their allegiance to the Federalists, and John Marshall, who had refused such bribes, was declared a hero. Nevertheless, this did not stop Benjamin Franklin Bache from labeling the president in his newspaper the "old, querulous, bald, blind, crippled, toothless Adams."[13]

Everyone thought John Adams would declare war against France immediately. He did not. He had promised American citizens to remain neutral, and he remained a man of his word.

ALIEN AND SEDITION ACTS

Days before Congress adjourned in July 1798, war had not been declared but an act was passed that would be the undoing of John Adams's presidency, though neither he nor Abigail thought so at the time. The Alien and Sedition

Acts—four bills passed into law in 1798 and signed by President Adams—allowed the federal government to strike back against any criticism or suspected disloyalty. According to three Alien acts, the United States government, after a declaration of war, was allowed to round up any men from an enemy nation over the age of 14 and detain them. The Sedition Act imposed fines and imprisonment for any person who "shall write, print, utter, or publish . . . any false, scandalous and malicious writing or writings against the government of the United States, or either house of the Congress of the United States, or the President of the United States."[14] Supporters of the laws said they would protect the country from enemy attacks; opponents, like the Republicans, believed they were intended to stifle criticisms of the Adams administration, particularly criticisms about the administration's conduct toward France.

Abigail wholeheartedly supported the measures, particularly the Sedition Act. She only wished it had gone further. According to Cokie Roberts, "If she had had her way, every newspaperman who criticized her husband would be thrown in jail, so when the Alien and Sedition Acts were passed and signed Abigail still wasn't satisfied."[15]

Upon returning to Quincy, Abigail fell ill. Nabby came to help care for her and stayed for weeks. It was serious this time, but Abigail survived. While she was recuperating, politics went on as usual. Abigail was frustrated being so far away; while she was in Philadelphia she had sources in the cabinet who kept her advised. She was missing more than she knew. Vice President Jefferson and James Madison were upset about the Alien and Sedition Acts and drafted a resolution declaring that a state could nullify a federal law. She was angry when she heard that some were trying to undo the Alien and Sedition Acts, which she said were "the two strongest barriers which the friends of the government have erected for their security and that of the public."[16]

Her feelings were so strong that she lost awareness of how central free expression was to democracy.

When it was time for John to return to Philadelphia, he once again left Abigail behind. Yet it was not long before Abigail was writing to John that he was not providing enough information. Shortly after returning to the capital, John wrote that their son Thomas was back from Europe after four-and-a-half years, and that cheered her. Their old friend Elbridge Gerry had also returned from France and informed John that the French wanted to negotiate. John had enough faith in him to send him back and thus preserve peace with France. Of the president and his wife, it was Abigail who had lobbied for war with France. There were mutterings among Federalists who were unhappy with their president's decision to negotiate. They wished "the old woman had been there."[17] Federalist New England was ready to go to war, as was Abigail. Alexander Hamilton was promoting war in the cabinet. John remained steadfast, however, in refusing to go to war.

FAMILY WORRIES

Because President Adams was in Quincy during the spring and summer of 1799, the Republicans accused him of neglecting the country's business, and in his absence, they began plotting against him. His return trip brought worries of a more personal nature. He stopped to visit Nabby in New York and also saw Charles's wife and children. Charles, however, was nowhere to be found. It was no secret now that the charming and handsome Charles was an alcoholic and was squandering his life. John wrote Abigail that he was renouncing him. Nabby's husband wasn't much better. John thought of him as a phony and a failure. He wondered if he should not have stayed home with his children instead of being away from them so much. Abigail wrote him, "You have the satisfaction of knowing that you have faithfully served your generation, that you have done it at the expense of all private considerations and you do not know whether you would have been a happier man in private than you have been in public life."[18]

In Philadelphia, the president learned that a move was out to deny him a second term. Because Alexander Hamilton and other members of his cabinet had joined the critics, he became pessimistic about being reelected in 1800. At the same time, plans were then in process to move the government to the new capital being built on the Potomac River, which would be named after George Washington. Abigail arrived in Philadelphia in mid-November, bringing with her Nabby and her five-year-old daughter, Caroline. Thomas was also with them.

On the first day Congress met, President Adams stood before the members and explained his reasoning for the mission to France. The reception was better than he had thought it would be. Then, in December 1799, George Washington died suddenly of a throat ailment. The death of the former president made many people conclude that Adams was not nearly as good a leader as Washington had been. Nevertheless, Abigail hosted a reception for 200 people after the funeral.

As 1800 dawned, the year of the fourth presidential election, Abigail worried about her husband's chances since there were divisions even within his own party. By the time Congress reconvened in May, two Federalists had been nominated for president, John Adams and Charles Pinckney, and Thomas Jefferson and Aaron Burr had been nominated for the Republicans. The pro-Republican newspaper attacks on Adams were vicious, with Jefferson stooping so low as to pay James Callender, a journalist, to print a steady stream of anti-Adams propaganda.

Abigail needed to prepare to move to the new seat of government, Washington, whether John won or lost.

Leaving Philadelphia made her sad. She did not think Washington the appropriate place for the new government. After she held a farewell drawing room reception in May and the family furniture was shipped, Abigail went home to Quincy. On the way she made the traditional stop in New York to see Charles and Nabby. William Smith was without a job again, a huge source of concern for Abigail. Charles had not sobered up; Abigail took his oldest child, a daughter named Susan, home with her. She left her family there with great sorrow in her heart.

President Adams went south to have a look at the construction in Washington. He was impressed. He also paid a call on Martha Washington, who later called Jefferson, his opponent in the election of 1800, "one of the most detestable of mankind."[19] As the campaign continued to heat up, it was as vicious as Abigail had predicted it would be. Perhaps John and Abigail's worst enemy was Alexander Hamilton. Resentful that Adams had not appointed him to the positions he had sought, he wrote a 54-page attack on the president.

During the electoral battle, Abigail wrote John Quincy to return home, as she worried about his future as a diplomat if a Republican won the election. She wanted people to see what he was up to. Cokie Roberts writes, "Her children were never too old or too important for Abigail Adams to try to run their lives."[20]

John Adams spent his first night in the new White House on November 1, 1800. He wrote to Abigail, "I pray Heaven to bestow the best of blessings on this House and all that shall hereafter inhabit it. May none but honest and wise men ever rule under this roof."[21] These words were later inscribed above the fireplace of the State Dining Room in the White House. Abigail began her journey to Washington, stopping in New York to check on family there. Charles, broken by his alcoholism, was on his deathbed. There was nothing she could do.

A portrait of Thomas Jefferson, after a painting by Gilbert Stuart. Although Jefferson and John Adams became great political rivals after working together to ensure American independence, their friendship would rekindle in their later years.

John was certain that he would lose the election. Happy that Abigail was joining him, he wrote her that "it was fit and proper that you and I should retire together."[22] She stopped in Philadelphia and continued on to Washington. Unimpressed by the new capital, she was determined to keep her criticism to herself and her immediate family. The presidential electors cast their votes on December 3, and on that same day Abigail and John learned that Charles was dead. Abigail said, "He was no man's enemy but his own."[23]

Then good news arrived. A treaty with France had been signed. John had to keep the news secret, as he had not received official word from his ministers. He wrote to a friend later, "I desire no other inscription over my gravestone than: 'Here lies John Adams, who took upon himself the responsibility of peace with France in the year 1800.'"[24]

Despite his success with maintaining the peace, John Adams would lose the presidential election. Not until late December would it be learned that the election was a tie, and as a result, would be decided by the House of Representatives. Jefferson had received 73 votes, Aaron Burr 73, Adams 65, and Pinckney 64. John Jay received one vote.

John and Abigail held the first New Year's reception at the White House. Abigail was disappointed in the results of the election, but she was clear that what she wanted most was the preservation of the government. It was especially upsetting that Jefferson might be replacing her husband as president, but she and John invited him to dinner with a group of congressmen. She, along with everyone else, remained in suspense, as there was a deadlock in the House, which was controlled by the Federalist Party. Most Federalists voted for Burr in order to prevent Jefferson from becoming president. Alexander Hamilton, a Federalist who hated both presidential frontrunners but preferred Jefferson to Burr, intervened on Jefferson's behalf. It was the representative from Maryland, Joseph Nicholson, almost too ill to lift a pen, who broke the deadlock. Jefferson was the new president.

Retirement Years

A bigail, concerned about road conditions, had departed Washington before the final results were in. The journey north was difficult. When the carriage arrived at the Susquehanna River, Abigail's traveling group decided to experiment to see how much weight the ice would bear. Her niece, Louisa Smith, begged her aunt to turn back when the ice started breaking near shore. Abigail said that she could handle the situation, since she was "accustomed to get through many a trying scene and combat many difficulties alone."[1] The comment reveals a woman in middle age who, though frail in body, was still a force to be reckoned with.

Although he had lost the election, President Adams was busy creating a judiciary bill that would allow him to appoint a group of last-minute judges, which made Jefferson, as the incoming president, furious. When Abigail heard what her husband was doing, she wanted to see the list he had come up with and contribute names of her own. John spent his final days in office naming a number of friends and family members to various positions. He also called his son John Quincy home from Berlin before Jefferson had the opportunity to do so. Although Abigail and Jefferson had had tea before she departed Washington, it would take more than a social get-together to heal the rift.

RETIREMENT

After leaving office in March 1801, Adams experienced waves of dejection and bitterness as he dealt with his new status over the next months. Charles's death, his unpopularity among some citizens, and the sudden seclusion after being a longstanding public figure were all hard on him. Abigail, on the other hand, had her husband home fulltime for the first time in decades and was content. Away from politics, she threw herself into maintaining the farm and wrote her daughter that she was back to milking cows. In a letter to her son John Quincy's mother-in-law, she wrote about her garden. Their land totaled 600 acres now, and it was expected to sustain them again.

Both were excited to learn that John Quincy's wife, Louisa Catherine, had given birth to a baby boy in Berlin, named George Washington Adams. Abigail, however, fretted about them not naming the child after his own grandfather. With the Republicans in power, John Quincy had no choice but to start his career over as a lawyer in Boston when he returned to the United States. Charles's wife, Sally, and her two daughters went to live with Abigail and John; Louisa Smith was already there. Nabby and her three children then arrived for the summer. Sometimes there were as many as 20 people living under their roof, not to mention

Juno, the Newfoundland puppy Abigail acquired upon her return home.

John Quincy and family arrived on September 4, 1801, and moved in with Thomas. By the time her son arrived in Quincy, Abigail was ill, but thrilled to have him home. John Quincy went down to Washington to bring back Louisa Catherine, who had taken the baby to visit her family there. Louisa, who had been raised in London and France, took an instant dislike to Quincy. Everyone in the town was a little in awe of the elegant woman, who grew irritated over their determination to entertain her and fuss over her. Abigail found her 26-year-old daughter-in-law terribly frail and worried that "she will be of short duration."[2]

By Christmas 1801, John Quincy had moved his wife and baby to a house in Boston. Months later, in April 1802, he was elected to the Massachusetts state senate. Although busy with his political career, he remained a dutiful son, riding out to Quincy nearly every weekend to visit his parents. After helping them through a financial crisis, he made the decision to move to Quincy. Another son, John, was born in 1803. In February 1803, John Quincy was elected a United States senator from Massachusetts. After the election, he moved to Washington.

Abigail and John, though generally critical of Jefferson, found it hard, in Abigail's words, "to discard him."[3] In 1804, they learned that his daughter Polly, who had spent time with them in London and France, had died. Abigail sat down and wrote her old friend a letter expressing her heartache and sympathy. She had not written him in 17 years. She was careful to sign her letter not as a friend but as one "who once took pleasure in subscribing herself your friend."[4] Jefferson responded from the President's House, as the White House was then known, expressing his regret that circumstances had divided them. Seven letters were exchanged, through which both aired their grievances.

Jefferson was angry that Adams made the "midnight appointments" to the judiciary. Abigail found it difficult to forgive him for supporting the journalist James Callender, who had publicly slandered her husband. She also could not let it go that Jefferson had replaced John Quincy as a commissioner of bankruptcy in Boston when he needed the job. What their correspondence boiled down to was a series of personal hurts that could not be completely forgiven.

Adams, however, refused to criticize President Jefferson in writing. He wrote, "I think instead of opposing systematically any administration, running down their characters and opposing all their measures, right or wrong, we ought to support every administration as far as we can in justice."[5]

At the same time the retired president was enjoying his new writing life, John and Abigail's old friend Mercy Warren published her book *History of the Rise, Progress, and Termination of the American Revolution,* in which she singled out Adams as the one who had betrayed the American Revolution. This time John did not hold back as he wrote his critic a series of letters defending his actions as president and expressing his anger. He and Abigail thought, sadly, that it marked the end of another friendship. John went on to write letters of indignation and self-defense to a newspaper called the *Boston Patriot* over a three-year period, until finally he realized that his efforts were fruitless.

THE BIG HOUSE

During this period of furious letter writing, John renewed his correspondence with his fellow signer of the Declaration of Independence, Dr. Benjamin Rush, an exchange that fed him intellectually. At the same time, Abigail remained involved with her children and grandchildren. She started a tradition of serving Sunday dinners at one o'clock at the "big house." A cousin of Abigail's, Josiah Quincy, recalled

Pictured above, the home of John and Abigail Adams in Massachusetts. This house would be home to five generations of their family. Abigail designed its gardens after ones she had seen during her time in Europe.

the matriarch: "She was always dressed handsomely, and her rich silks and laces seemed appropriate to a lady of her dignified position in the town. . . . The aristocratic colonial families were still recognized, for the tide of democracy had not risen high enough to cover all its distinctions."[6]

Her children, however, remained a concern. Although she liked that John Quincy was following in his father's footsteps, she and his wife, Louisa Catherine, lived a life of compromise, as Louisa was not interested in sacrificing the way her mother-in-law had for her husband's political career. She wanted to be with her husband or with her own family. At the same time, Thomas was not faring well in Philadelphia, and his brother talked him into moving back north to Quincy. He made his mother promise to leave Thomas alone and not offer him advice, as she was prone to do at the slightest instigation.

In the summer of 1805, Thomas married Nancy Harrod and they moved in with Abigail and John. Fortunately, Nancy and Abigail got along very well. Because Thomas had failed at the law, he became the caretaker of his parents' property. He drank heavily and was often extremely unpleasant to be around.

Although she spent most of her time being concerned about her children, Abigail continued to follow politics but was not as emotionally involved in it as in the past. In order to keep her family near her, she had an addition built onto their house; the sons of John Quincy and Louisa remained with Abigail while their parents were in Washington. At the same time, John Quincy's older son, George, boarded with Abigail's sister, just as her children had done. Louisa Catherine hated the arrangement, but felt overpowered by her husband and his mother. When she wrote how much she missed her children, Abigail chided her that it was important to consider the children's best interests. After the first year in Washington, Louisa Catherine chose to remain behind with her children.

A family crisis occurred when Nabby's husband, William Smith, became embroiled in a scheme to free the people of Colombia from Spanish rule. Since Smith was the surveyor of the port of New York, he could not become directly involved in the plan; instead, he sent his son William to Colombia early in 1806. Though they tried to hide the adventure from Abigail, she soon learned that the leader of this enterprise and his men were arrested, and the older William was arrested for his part in the expedition. The son, however, managed to escape. Although Nabby's husband was eventually acquitted, he was unable to support his family after his trial. Abigail worried constantly about her daughter's family and finally persuaded John Quincy to stop in New York and talk Nabby into coming to Quincy. Nabby's husband went to upstate New York to farm, and Nabby and her daughter Caroline went to Quincy.

All the while, the Adams family was growing. Thomas and his wife had a baby whom they named Elizabeth. Louisa Catherine and John Quincy had a third son, Charles Francis. At a dinner a week before John Quincy was to head back to Washington, Abigail had more of her family around her than ever before. All her children were there, and 16 grandchildren. Abigail wanted to keep Nabby and 12-year-old Caroline with her for the winter, but when William Smith came to fetch them, she let them go.

POLITICAL CHANGE

France and England were still at war when Thomas Jefferson began his second term as president in 1805; Napoleon Bonaparte had crowned himself emperor of France a few months earlier, and his armies would dominate Europe for almost a decade to come. At the same time, the Federalist Party was growing increasingly unpopular at home. By the winter of 1808, the party had grown so feeble that John Quincy attended a Republican caucus to choose candidates for the upcoming presidential election. Abigail was shocked to read that her son had gone, but she hoped that President Jefferson would reward John Quincy for his conversion.

Although Jefferson gave her son nothing, the next president was more generous. This was James Madison, Jefferson's old ally and the Republicans' choice for president in 1808. Abigail also supported Madison, in large part because the Federalists had become more and more pro-British. In 1809, President Madison appointed John Quincy ambassador to Russia, and Abigail's son

A late-eighteenth century tinted engraved portrait of Abigail Adams. Although she devoted her attention to her family in her later years, Abigail kept abreast of politics.

prepared to set off with Louisa and Charles Francis. Now John joined Abigail in her dismay that their beloved oldest son would be away a minimum of three years. They had become accustomed to his regular visits. Abigail was so upset that, just as with her husband in years past, she refused to see her son off.

WAVES OF GRIEF

In 1811, Abigail, after learning how unhappy John Quincy and Louisa Catherine were in Russia, wrote a personal appeal to President Madison to bring them home. Madison in turn offered John Quincy an appointment to the Supreme Court, but to his mother's dismay John Quincy turned it down. Despite his and his wife's unhappiness, he felt that he could better serve his country in the Russian czar's court. Also, because his wife was again pregnant, he did not want to subject her to the 6,000-mile journey. Abigail worried that she might never see him again. She wrote, "At the advanced years both of his Father and Myself, we can have very little expectation of meeting again upon this mortal theater."[7]

Around the same time, Abigail's family became troubled by poor health. First, Thomas was thrown from a horse and was so badly injured that Abigail and John worried that he would be crippled for life. In September, John fell over a stick and ripped his leg open and was confined to the house. Then Abigail's sister Mary became ill, and Abigail went back and forth between houses caring for her family. That same year it was discovered that Nabby had a rapidly growing tumor in one breast. She went to Boston to see a doctor, who diagnosed cancer but did not prescribe treatment. She went to her father's old friend Benjamin Rush in Philadelphia, and he urged her to have surgery. Nabby underwent the removal of the entire breast on October 8, 1811, and she was pronounced cured. She went to Quincy to recuperate under her mother's care.

A week after the surgery, Abigail's beloved sister Mary and her husband, Richard Cranch, died on successive days. Richard was 85 and Mary was 70. Abigail was overcome with sadness. John Quincy's sons, who were living with them, went to Abigail's other sister, Elizabeth, to attend her husband's academy.

Abigail turned 68 on November 22, 1812. Considering all the difficulties her family had recently endured, she thought it miraculous that she and John were both doing well. Then, in January 1813, she received a letter from John Quincy that his 13-month-old baby girl, who looked liked Abigail, had died. Louisa Catherine was overcome

DEATH OF NABBY

Nabby Adams Smith was diagnosed with breast cancer in 1811 at the age of 47. She underwent a mastectomy on October 11. The only anesthetic used was opium, but Nabby endured the ordeal with fortitude. The surgeons declared her cured. She went to Quincy to recuperate, and the following summer returned to her home in upstate New York. Throughout the following winter she went to the doctor for severe pain and was diagnosed as having rheumatism, but by the spring of 1813 she knew the cancer had returned. Her husband, Colonel William Smith, went to Congress, leaving the couple's 18-year-old daughter, Caroline, to care for her mother. Abigail had thought she would never see her daughter again, as travel seemed out of the question.

But Nabby wanted to go home to be with her mother. She was in unbearable pain, but her children honored her wish. It took two weeks to travel from upstate New York to Braintree. They arrived in July and she died on August 15, leaving behind three children, Caroline, John, and William, who was in Russia serving as secretary to John Quincy.

with grief; though religious, she did not have the faith that seemed to carry Abigail through the worst crises.

When Nabby started experiencing unremitting pain in 1813, all feared the worst. It was soon known that the cancer had returned. Though Nabby had been unable to get across her room, she insisted on going to her mother's to die. Abigail welcomed her daughter and her children when they arrived in July. Nabby's husband, William, arrived from Washington; a week later she declared that her time had come. Nabby

Abigail had never imagined having to endure Nabby's death. She wrote John Quincy, "The wound which has lacerated my Bosom cannot be healed. The broken Heart may be bound up; and religion teach submission and silence, even under the anguish of the Heart, but it cannot cure it. The unbidden sigh will rise, and the bitter tear flow long after the Tomb is closed."[*]

Abigail wrote obsessively about Nabby after her death, repeating over and over to friends and family, including John Quincy and Mercy Warren, the story of the cancer, the operation, and Nabby's death. She wrote about Nabby's goodness and her passage to a better life. For the first time she expressed loss of hope, but eventually, through her strong faith and devotion to the rest of her family, she began to heal. Caroline was a consolation, as she was a constant reminder of her mother. Abigail wrote of her granddaughter, "All that I can wish for, she is."[**]

[*] Akers, p. 211.
[**] Cokie Roberts, *Ladies of Liberty: The Women Who Shaped Our Nation*. New York: William Morrow, 2008, p. 259.

asked the family to sing a hymn, "Longing for Heaven." She died a few hours later at age 48. Abigail went into a state of despair; her daughter had been her closest companion. It was inconceivable that she was dead. John was 77 and asked his old friend Benjamin Rush how many more deaths he would have to endure, how many aches and pains.

Deaths in the family seemed to be coming in quick succession. Abigail had lost one sister. Her niece Elizabeth Cranch Norton had died, along with one of Thomas's sons and the infant daughter of John Quincy. Sally Adams, the widow of her son Charles, had lain at death's door but managed to recover. Yet despite all her sorrows, Abigail could write to her son in October of the blessings still left to her.

WAR AND PEACE

In the meantime, Benjamin Rush wrote to remind John that two brothers from Virginia, who had paid a call on John, had returned to Virginia and to Monticello, the home of Jefferson, and told him that John Adams had said in conversation, "I always loved Jefferson and I still love him."[8] Jefferson had written to Rush, "I only needed this knowledge to revive towards him all the affections of the most cordial moments of our lives."[9] John wrote Jefferson a note on New Year's Day, 1812. Jefferson sent a warm reply back immediately, and a correspondence developed. John wrote to Rush and told him that he had "wrought wonders!"[10] Of the exchange between the two former revolutionaries and presidents, David McCullough writes, "Within months a half dozen letters had traveled the roads between Quincy and Monticello, and one of the most extraordinary correspondences in American history—indeed, in the English language—was under way."[11]

While Jefferson and Adams renewed their friendship, war was on the horizon. The resulting war between the United States and Great Britain, the War of 1812, grew out of the struggle between Britain and Napoleon, who then controlled most of Europe. In order to weaken Napoleon's grip on the continent, the British harassed any ships that attempted to trade with Europe. The ships included American ships, which led to a series of confrontations between the United States and Britain. The British had also provoked the United States by forcing its sailors to work on British ships and by refusing to withdraw from American territory along the Great Lakes. Additionally, the British were backing Native American tribes against the Americans and refused to sign commercial agreements.

On June 12, 1812, President James Madison asked Congress to declare war on Britain. When war broke out, most of the fighting took place along the Canadian border, along the Gulf of Mexico, and in the Chesapeake Bay area. The United States was not prepared for war, and many Americans were opposed to the conflict. Abigail, however, believed strongly that this war was essential to preserve America's hard-won independence.

Meanwhile, in Europe, Napoleon was leading a great army into Russia. Abigail and John read everything they could get their hands on about world events. Before the year was out, John Quincy had written to his parents that the French conqueror had managed to take Moscow, deep in the Russian heartland. The victory, however, did Napoleon little good. He had no food for his troops, and when winter came on he had to turn them around and march them home, this time through deadly cold and snow. His army disintegrated. Now Europe knew he could be beaten; in less than two years he would no longer be emperor.

Napoleon stepped down as French emperor in April 1814. That same month, John Quincy learned he had been appointed as a peace envoy and was being sent to Ghent,

Belgium, for negotiations to end America's war with Britain. The conflict still had some final eruptions. On August 24, the British attacked Washington and set fire to the Capitol and to the President's House.

The Treaty of Ghent, which ended the war, was signed in December 1814. John Quincy wrote his mother first with the news, but his success did not bring him home. Instead, he was appointed minister to Great Britain. Because of this appointment, it was time for Abigail and John to part with their two beloved grandsons, George and John, who were joining their parents overseas after a six-year separation. Abigail loved reading John Quincy's accounts of their activities in London.

Abigail's sister Elizabeth died suddenly in 1815. Abigail wrote that she heard a "loud call . . . to live in a habitual preparation for a summons to depart."[12] Her hope of seeing John Quincy again kept her hope alive. Abigail wrote her will, leaving her silk gowns and jewelry, beds and blankets and $4,000 to children, grandchildren, and her niece, Louisa Smith. Her two sons were to divide the land she had inherited.

Abigail's dream of a reunion with her son John Quincy and his family came true in 1817. After James Monroe had been reelected president, John Quincy Adams was appointed secretary of state. McCullough writes, "In the history of the Adams family there was probably no more joyous homecoming than took place in the heart of midmorning on August 18, 1817, when John Quincy, Louisa Catherine, and their three sons came over the hill from Milton in a coach-and-four trailing a cloud of dust."[13] John Quincy was 50. He had served as minister to the Netherlands and Prussia, U.S. senator, Harvard professor, and minister to Russia and Great Britain, and he was soon to be secretary of state. As three presidents—Jefferson, Madison, and Monroe—had first served as secretaries of state, many thought his destiny was to become president.

The months that followed their son's return were the happiest of their retirement years. Abigail wrote regularly to John Quincy and Louisa Catherine about the changing seasons. They returned for a vacation, and visitors to the house found Abigail sitting on the couch sorting laundry or shelling beans. People loved to hear her stories.

In October, Abigail became ill with typhoid fever. Adams wrote Jefferson, "The dear partner of my life for fifty-four years as a wife, and for many years more as a lover, now lies in extremis, forbidden to speak or be spoken to."[14] She was 74 and all were worried that she might not be able to bounce back as she had in the past. On October 26, she spoke for the first time. She told her beloved husband that she was dying and that "if it was the will of Heaven, she was ready. She had no wish to live except for his sake."[15] John announced to friends gathered that he wished he could lie down beside her and die too.

Abigail Adams died on October 28, 1818, at around one o'clock in the afternoon. Her son Thomas said she seemed conscious until her last breath. She was buried on November 1 at the First Unitarian Church in Quincy. For her funeral, John insisted on walking in the procession, though he was then over 80 years old.

John Quincy did not learn of his mother's death until a day after the funeral. He wrote in his diary, "My mother . . . was a minister of blessing to all human beings within her sphere of action . . . She had no feelings but of kindness and beneficence. Yet her mind was as firm as her temper was mild and gentle. She . . . has been to me more than a mother . . . Never have I known another human being, the perpetual object of whose life, was so unremittingly to do good."[16]

An 1826 oil-on-canvas portrait of John Adams done by Gilbert Stuart during the president's late retirement.

Abigail had signed her last letter to Jefferson, "your
old and steady friend." Jefferson wrote John, "Tried myself
in the school of affliction, by the loss of every form of

connection which can rive the human heart, I know well, and feel what you have lost, what you have suffered, and are suffering, and have yet to endure."[17] John Adams would live another eight years, until the age of 90, and he and Jefferson would die on the same day, July 4, 1826—the fiftieth anniversary of the Declaration of Independence.

Her Legacy

In the foreword to *My Dearest Friend: Letters of Abigail and John Adams,* the historian Joseph J. Ellis writes of Abigail's significance as a first lady, "Before there was Eleanor Roosevelt or Hillary Clinton, there was Abigail Adams."[1] Known for being shy and stubborn as a child, and opinionated and outspoken as an adult, Abigail Adams became both a domestic and political partner to her husband, John Adams, in a marriage that lasted over a half century. Abigail, unlike her predecessor, Martha Washington, formed a team with her husband, one in which she was his chief adviser and confidante.

The approximately 1,160 letters she and John Adams wrote came to light for the first time in 1876 when their grandson Charles Francis Adams, son of John Quincy and Louisa Catherine, published *Familiar Letters of John Adams and His Wife, During the Revolution*. In 1956, the Massachusetts Historical Society began a commitment to publish a modern edition of the letters. Whereas Charles Francis altered the letters, leaving out what he considered trivial information, Lyman H. Butterfield changed nothing but punctuation. The letters covered the most important 40 years of American history, when, according to Ellis, "the core values [of America] were declared and the abiding institutions created."[2] The literary quality of the letters shines alongside their value as historical documents. Letters of the eighteenth and nineteenth centuries, unlike e-mails, were crafted compositions. Letter writing was an art form, and taken quite seriously. The American public today can be grateful that was the case.

Abigail would no doubt have been amazed to find her letters having as much significance as her husband's 150 years after her death. Her biographer Lynne Withey writes, "Yet surely she would have approved of the reasons for her fame: the interest of a later age in the history of family and domestic life, as well as the history of politics; and above all, its interest in the emancipation of women

DID YOU KNOW?

During her lifetime, Abigail Adams was approached for permission to publish some of her political letters but she refused. She considered it improper for a woman's private correspondence to be publicly displayed. When her letters were published decades after her death by her grandson, she became the first presidential wife to have her writings printed for the general public.

and in the discovery of women in the past who spoke out on behalf of their sex."[3]

THE CHILDREN

Ellis writes, "They [Abigail and John] regarded their children and the enduring American republic as their greatest legacies."[4] Their four children were the source of great pride and equal disappointment. Both Charles and Thomas succumbed to alcohol. "Tommy" was the father of seven children and died at the age of 60, six years after his father. Abigail and John did everything in their power to help Nabby, whose husband was a failure. In addition to suffering the loss of a stillborn child, Abigail had to endure the death of three of their children, Susanna at 13 months, Charles from alcoholism, and Nabby from cancer. It was their son John Quincy in whom they placed all their hopes and dreams for the future, and he did not let them down. He was chosen president of the United States in 1824. Abigail was the first and only woman to be both wife and mother of American presidents, and held that position until Barbara Bush, wife to George H. W. Bush and mother to George W. Bush, could say the same.

Abigail understood early in her marriage that sacrifice would be required in order for her husband to fulfill his destiny of having a voice in the creation of a new nation. She never had regrets, though she was the first to admit that the long separations from John were the greatest trial of her life. Feisty even as a child, she was always the greatest defender of her husband's actions, displaying fury when he was attacked. Even after she and John had retired to Quincy, she took a firm stand in support of the War of 1812, which went against the opinions of most New Englanders.

THE CHANGING ROLE OF WOMEN

It is common for biographers of women to speculate on how their subjects would fit into the modern era, how their talents might have been used in today's world. One writer thinks Abigail would perhaps be a novelist or a memoirist; another imagines her as a feminist. She had great compassion for women who were in difficult marriages, and was humble about her good fortune to be married to a man who held her in high respect. She witnessed her daughter's less-than-perfect marriage, yet she firmly believed that a woman's role was to be a helpmate to her husband. She believed that "the die once cast, there is no retreat until death."[5]

Women of her era could not own property; even the clothes they wore and the jewelry belonged to their husbands. Abigail did not like the notion of women being subjugated to men. She thought a woman should be able to limit the number of children she had, and she refused to believe that women were intellectually inferior to men. She fervently believed in virtue, and that it was up to mothers to instill in their sons patriotism and public service that might involve sacrifices. She lived that creed, first accepting the long separations from her husband, and later keeping watch over John Quincy's sons while their parents were away.

She had started promoting education for women as early as 1776, and it was her continuing goal to see more educated women. She knew that was the key to their emancipation. In 1778, after John and John Quincy sailed for Europe, she wrote to her cousin John Thaxter, who was working as a secretary to Congress, that she had wanted to go but John did not consider it prudent. In asking him to provide her with information about politics and current events, she wrote, "It is really mortifying, Sir, when a woman possessed of a common share of understanding considers the difference of education between the male and female sex."[6]

It was the American Revolution, when women had to step into nontraditional roles, that helped contribute to a new demand for equal education. Benjamin Rush helped

A statue of Abigail Adams with her son John Quincy Adams. It stands outside the family's church in Quincy, Massachusetts.

establish one of the first schools for girls, the Young Ladies Academy of Philadelphia, in 1787. Later, when Abigail was first lady, she enrolled her 10-year-old granddaughter in a school in New York that taught arithmetic, geography, French, and English. In 1790, Mercy Warren began publishing books under her own name. She was not alone; other female writers were coming onto the scene. For example, Mary Wollstonecraft's *Vindication of the Rights of Women* had arrived from England in 1792, calling for political and civil rights for women. Many more such treatises were to follow.

As much as anyone, through her counsel to her husband, and through her sacrifices, Abigail knew that she had taken a real part in the building of the American nation. Cokie Roberts, in *Founding Mothers: The Women Who Raised Our Nation*, writes: "I decided that there's nothing unique about them. They did—with great hardship, courage, pluck, prayerfulness, sadness, joy, energy, and humor—what women do. They put one foot in front of the other in remarkable circumstances. They carried on."[7]

Abigail Adams wrote when John Adams left public office, "I leave to time the unfolding of a drama. I leave to posterity to reflect upon the times past; and I leave them characters to contemplate."[8]

In November 2008, history was made when Barack Obama was elected as the first black president of the United States. In an article about Obama's remarkable election written for *U.S. News & World Report*, columnist David Gergen ended with a quotation from a letter Abigail Adams wrote to her son John Quincy during the Revolution:

These are the times in which a genius would wish to live. It is not in the still calm of life . . . that great characters are formed. The habits of a vigorous mind are found in contending with difficulties.

Great necessities call out great virtues, when a mind is raised, and animated by scenes that engage the heart, then those qualities which would otherwise lay dormant, wake into life and form the character of the hero and the statesman.[9]

Abigail Adams could have been writing about herself.

CHRONOLOGY

1744   Born Abigail Smith on November 22, [November 11, old style] in Weymouth, Massachusetts.

1759   Meets John Adams.

1764   Marries John Adams in Weymouth.

1765   Daughter Abigail (Nabby) is born.

1767   Son John Quincy is born.

1768   Daughter Susanna is born.

1770   Son Charles is born; Susanna dies in February.

1772   Son Thomas Boylston is born.

1774   John attends the Continental Congress in Philadelphia.

1775   Battles of Lexington and Concord; Abigail's mother, Elizabeth Quincy Smith, dies.

1776   Declaration of Independence signed.

1778   Abigail delivers a stillborn baby; John and John Quincy sail to France.

1779   John and John Quincy return to Boston. John, John Quincy, and Charles sail to Spain, then travel to Paris.

1780   John elected minister to the Netherlands.

1782   The Netherlands formally recognizes American independence.

1783   Peace treaty signed with Great Britain.

1784   Abigail and Nabby sail to England and then settle in France.

1785 John is chosen as first American minister to Great Britain.

1789 John is elected vice president under President George Washington.

1792 John is elected to second term as vice president under Washington.

1796 John is elected second president of the United States.

1800 Charles dies in New York City.

1801 John is defeated for reelection to the presidency by Thomas Jefferson.

1813 Nabby dies in Quincy.

1818 Abigail dies on October 28.

1826 John dies on July 4.

NOTES

CHAPTER 1: ONE WOMAN'S SACRIFICE

1. Charles W. Akers, *Abigail Adams: A Revolutionary American Woman*. New York: Pearson Longman, 2007, p. 40.
2. Cokie Roberts, *Founding Mothers: The Women Who Raised Our Nation*, New York: Harper Perennial, 2005, p. 70.
3. Akers, p. 32.
4. Roberts, p. 102.
5. Ibid., p. 174.

CHAPTER 2: A "SHY BUT OBSTINATE" CHILD

1. Lynne Withey, *Dearest Friend: A Life of Abigail Adams*. New York: Touchstone, 2002, p. 5.
2. Ibid, p. 9.
3. L.H. Butterfield, Marc Friedlaender, and Mary-Jo Kline, eds., *The Book of Abigail and John: Selected Letters of the Adams Family 1762–1784*. Cambridge, Mass.: Harvard University Press, 1975, p. 4.
4. Ibid.
5. Akers, p. 16.
6. David McCullough, *John Adams*. New York: Simon & Schuster Paperbacks, 2001, p. 52.

CHAPTER 3: BIRTHING A NATION

1. McCullough, p. 57.
2. Ibid., p. 56.
3. Akers, p. 22.
4. Ibid.
5. McCullough, p. 58.
6. Akers, p. 27.
7. McCullough, p. 59.
8. Withey, p. 38.
9. Akers, p. 23.

10. Withey, p. 30.
11. Ibid., p. 31.
12. Edith Belle Gelles, *Portia: The World of Abigail Adams*. Bloomington: Indiana University Press, 1995, p. 33.
13. Ibid.
14. McCullough, p. 129.
15. Ibid., p. 142.

CHAPTER 4: A LIFE IN LETTERS

1. McCullough, p. 144.
2. Ibid., p. 150–151.
3. Gelles, p. 5.
4. Akers, p. 26.
5. Ibid., p. 59.
6. Roberts, *Founding Mothers*, p. 102.
7. Gelles, p. 53.
8. Akers, p. 70.
9. McCullough, p. 257.
10. Ibid., p. 285.
11. Ibid., p. 286.

CHAPTER 5: QUEST FOR FAME

1. Withey, p. 149.
2. Akers, p. 85.
3. McCullough, p. 295.
4. Ibid., p. 297.
5. Ibid., p. 299.
6. Ibid., p. 312.
7. Ibid.
8. Ibid., p. 320.
9. Ibid., p. 325.
10. Akers, p. 102.
11. McCullough, p. 345.

12. Ibid., p. 346.
13. Ibid., p. 340.
14. Ibid., p. 362.
15. Ibid., p. 382.
16. Ibid., p. 385.
17. Akers, p. 123.

CHAPTER 6: THE VICE PRESIDENCY

1. McCullough, p. 392.
2. Ibid., p. 404.
3. Ibid., p. 413.
4. Akers, p. 141.
5. McCullough, p. 440.
6. Ibid., p. 458.
7. Ibid.
8. Ibid., p. 459.

CHAPTER 7: SECOND FIRST LADY

1. McCullough, p. 462.
2. Ibid., p. 465.
3. Ibid.
4. Ibid., p. 466.
5. Cokie Roberts, *Ladies of Liberty: The Women Who Shaped Our Nation*. New York: William Morrow, 2008, p. 9.
6. McCullough, p. 467.
7. Roberts, *Ladies of Liberty*, p. 9.
8. Ibid., p. 10.
9. Ibid., p. 14.
10. Ibid., p. 25.
11. Ibid., p. 27.
12. Ibid., p. 28.
13. Ibid., p. 26.
14. Ibid., pp. 29–30.

15. Ibid.
16. Ibid., p. 32.
17. Ibid., p. 34.
18. Ibid., p. 32.
19. Ibid., p. 41.
20. Ibid., p. 42.
21. Ibid.
22. Ibid.
23. Ibid., p. 44.
24. McCullough, p. 567.

CHAPTER 8: RETIREMENT YEARS

1. Roberts, *Ladies of Liberty*, p. 49.
2. McCullough, p. 575.
3. Ibid., p. 581.
4. Ibid.
5. Ibid., p. 594.
6. Ibid., p. 597.
7. Akers, p. 209.
8. McCullough, p. 602–603.
9. Ibid.
10. Ibid., p. 604.
11. Ibid., p. 605.
12. Akers, p. 212.
13. McCullough, p. 621.
14. Ibid., p. 622.
15. Ibid., p. 623.
16. Ibid., p. 624.
17. Phyllis Lee Levin, *Abigail Adams: A Biography*. New York: St. Martin's Press, 2001.

CHAPTER 9: HER LEGACY

1. Margaret A. Hogan and C. James Taylor, eds., *My Dearest Friend: Letters of Abigail and John Adams.*

Cambridge, Mass.: Belknap Press of Harvard University Press, 2007, p. x.

2. Ibid., p. vii.
3. Withey, p. 317.
4. Hogan and Taylor, p. xii.
5. Akers, p. 216.
6. Roberts, *Founding Mothers*, p. 149.
7. Ibid., p. xx.
8. Roberts, *Ladies of Liberty*, p. 394.
9. David Gergen, "At a Time of Crisis, Hope for the Future." *U.S. News & World Report*, December 1–8, 2008, p. 56.

BIBLIOGRAPHY

Akers, Charles W. *Abigail Adams: A Revolutionary American Woman*. New York: Pearson Longman, 2007.

Butterfield, L.H., Marc Friedlaender, and Mary-Jo Kline, eds. *The Book of Abigail and John: Selected Letters of the Adams Family, 1762–1784*. Cambridge, Mass.: Harvard University Press, 1975.

Dowd, Maureen. "The First Farmeress," *New York Times*, June 17, 2001. Available online at http://query/nytimes.com/gst/fullpage.html.

Gelles, Edith Belle. *Portia: The World of Abigail Adams*. Bloomington: Indiana University Press, 1995.

Gergen, David. "At a Time of Crisis, Hope for the Future." *U.S. News & World Report*, December 1–8, 2008, p. 56.

Hogan, Margaret A., and C. James Taylor, eds. *My Dearest Friend: Letters of Abigail and John Adams*. Cambridge, Mass.: Belknap Press of Harvard University Press, 2007.

Levin, Phyllis Lee. *Abigail Adams: A Biography*. New York: St. Martin's Press, 2001.

McCullough, David. *John Adams*. New York: Simon & Schuster, 2001.

Roberts, Cokie. *Founding Mothers: The Women Who Raised Our Nation*. New York: Harper Perennial, 2005.

———. *Ladies of Liberty: The Women Who Shaped Our Nation*. New York: William Morrow, 2008.

Withey, Lynne. *Dearest Friend: A Life of Abigail Adams*. New York: Touchstone, 2002.

FURTHER RESOURCES

BOOKS

Bober, Natalie. *Abigail Adams: Witness to a Revolution.* New York: Simon Pulse, 1998.

Davis, Kate. *Abigail Adams.* San Diego: Blackbirch Press, 2002.

Gelles, Edith B. *Abigail Adams: A Writing Life.* New York and London: Routledge, 2002.

Manera, Alexandria. *Abigail Adams.* Minneapolis, Minn.: Lake Street Publishers, 2003.

WEB SITES

Gale Cengage Learning: Abigail Adams
http://www.gale.cengage.com/free_resources/whm/bio/adams_a.htm

National First Ladies' Library
http://www.firstladies.org/curriculum

PBS American Experience: John & Abigail Adams
http://www.pbs.org/wgbh/amex/adams

White House: First Ladies
http:/www.whitehouse.gov/history/firstladies/aa2.html

PICTURE CREDITS

INDEX

ABOUT THE AUTHOR

JANET HUBBARD-BROWN, who started her career as a researcher at Time-Life Books, has written dozens of books for Chelsea House, including biographies of Ray Charles and Condoleezza Rice for the Black Americans of Achievement series, and biographies of Eleanor Roosevelt and Abigail Adams for the Women of Achievement series. Her next book will be a biography of Tina Fey.